Accomack-Northampton
Planning District Commission

Chincoteague National Wildlife Refuge
Alternative Transportation Study

Prepared by
Volpe National Transportation Systems Center
55 Broadway, Cambridge MA 02142
www.volpe.dot.gov

April 2010

Table of Contents

List of Maps

List of Figures

List of Tables

1 Introduction

The U.S. Fish and Wildlife Service (FWS) Chincoteague National Wildlife Refuge (CNWR) is located along Virginia's Eastern Shore in Accomack County. The CNWR is comprised of several barrier beach islands, of which the Virginia portion of Assateague Island is the largest and the subject of this study. The U.S. National Park Service (NPS) oversees the administration of the Assateague Island National Seashore (ASIS), which includes the entirety of Assateague Island, in both Virginia and Maryland. CNWR and the Virginia District of ASIS are accessible by road from the mainland via Chincoteague Island and the Town of Chincoteague. The popularity of Assateague Island's beach and other attractions, combined with its limited access and parking, has resulted in seasonal traffic congestion and other transportation concerns that affect CNWR and the surrounding area.

In early 2007, CNWR, in partnership with NPS, the Town of Chincoteague, Accomack County and the Accomack-Northampton Planning District Commission, submitted a planning grant application to the Federal Transit Administration's Alternative Transportation in Parks and Public Lands (ATPPL) program. The application sought funding to study alternative transportation options that could mitigate transportation issues on and between the CNWR and the Town of Chincoteague. The Federal Transit Administration approved the grant and the partners received funding for the study in the fall of 2007, subsequently selecting the U.S. Department of Transportation's Volpe National Transportation Systems Center to carry out the alternative transportation study.

Purpose and Need

The ATPPL proposal stated that transportation planning for the future is essential, because, while there have been incremental improvements in vehicular access, parking, and accommodation for pedestrians and bicyclists, current and future demand will outstrip these improvements. The proposal's stated objectives of the project are to:

- Improve access, transportation safety, and visitor experience;

- Reduce traffic congestion;

- Minimize adverse effects of the transportation system to the natural environment within CNWR, including portions managed by the National Park Service (NPS), and within the adjacent Town of Chincoteague; and

- Improve financial and management sustainability at CNWR and ASIS.

The ATPPL grant proposal described several major transportation issues that occur primarily during the summer peak visitation season. Serious traffic congestion frequently occurs along Main Street and Maddox Boulevard in the Town of Chincoteague, and on the main access road through CNWR to ASIS. The resulting traffic delays adversely affect visitor experiences in CNWR and ASIS, as well as in the Town of Chincoteague, and prevent the timely arrival of CNWR and ASIS employees at their destinations to complete work assignments.

The congestion also poses a safety issue, as it can block access of law enforcement and ambulance personnel in case of an emergency and prevent quick and orderly egress of beachgoers when sudden storms hit the area. The safety of visitors arriving via pedestrian and bicycle modes is a special concern, as the designated paths are incomplete in some places, do not meet standards in other places, and do not always provide safe barriers from vehicles. Thus bicycles and pedestrians are often intermixed with vehicular traffic, at times during peak traffic conditions.

Finally, vehicular traffic in CNWR and ASIS causes toxins and pollutants to enter the soils and wetlands adjacent to the roads and parking areas. These adjacent waters, salt marshes and wetlands support marine life and vegetation that are very sensitive to pollutants, as do the nearby bay and ocean ecosystems, which are the ultimate receptors of these substances.

In addition to these issues explicitly cited in the ATPPL application, CNWR, ASIS, and FWS Regional staff have identified the related and important issue of the sustainability of the public beach parking lots, which are the destination of the majority of visitors' automobiles entering CNWR. These lots are located directly adjacent to the ocean beaches along the southern end of CNWR's jurisdiction, occupy important shorebird nesting and foraging habitat, and frequently sustain serious storm and wave damage requiring significant and expensive repairs. The management of beach parking is thus a confluence of essential transportation and environmental planning objectives.

In November 2009, Nor'easter Ida, a storm of historical significance, struck CNWR and ASIS and again demonstrated the vulnerability of the public beach parking lots and other infrastructure. A preliminary assessment of the storm's impact included:

- Damage roughly estimated at $600,000-$900,000 to the public beach parking lots, which have been washed away and/or buried under three feet of sand (Figure 1)

- Tidal overwash of part of Assateague Island such that Toms Cove Hook is now detached during high tide and connected only by a narrow sand bar during low tide

- Beach Road experienced heavy overwash due to storm surge and beach overwash. Flooding of the Refuge impoundment put significant hydraulic pressure on Beach Road, which then experienced weeping, which has undermined the road's structural stability (Figure 2)

The storm closed CNWR and ASIS for several days and limited access to the beach, trails, and other areas for some time thereafter.

Figure 1. Turn Circle at CNWR Beach Post-Storm, November 2009.

Source: CNWR website; photo credit: James Fair; November 2009.

Figure 2. Beach Road Post-Storm, November 2009.

Source: CNWR website; photo credit: James Fair; November 2009.

Background

Scope of ATPPL Application

The work program described in the approved ATPPL application is a "comprehensive transportation planning study", whose main points are the following:

- "Assess current deficiencies, problem areas, safety issues, and transportation needs; and,

- "Explore and propose the best motorized and non-motorized alternative transportation systems to alleviate traffic congestion and enhance visitor safety" in the project area, to maximize efficiency and use of roadways, parking lots and bicycle and pedestrian paths".

This report addresses the first point in its description of existing conditions and by review of comments from CNWR and ASIS staff and the public, the latter through the outreach process described in Chapter 4. The development of alternative transportation systems is based on the review of related plans and analyses (Chapter 3), examination of similar sites and transportation solutions (Chapter 5), and assessment of current and prospective transportation partners in the study area. Finally, the scope of the alternatives is fully developed through description of various implementation factors and the alternatives are assessed according to a set of criteria reviewed and approved by CNWR.

Program Input

The approval of the ATPPL proposal is, in part, a recognition that CNWR has been engaged over the long term in a management and planning process in which transportation is a critical issue. CNWR, along with its co-applicants, participated in an ATPPL Interagency Transportation Assistance Group (TAG), conducted January 8-10, 2008. The TAG's recommendations for action were substantively incorporated into the ATPPL application and, subsequently, the scope of work for this study (summary of issues and solutions identified as part of the TAG appears in Appendix A). CNWR is now updating its 1993 *Master*

Plan with a Comprehensive Conservation Plan (CCP), the primary visioning and management tool for all national wildlife refuges and ASIS has also begun updating its General Management Plan. Both will address access and transportation.

1. *CNWR Master Plan (1993)*

The CNWR *Master Plan*, which predates the requirement for a Comprehensive Conservation Plan, outlines the history and mission of CNWR. It includes the following directives for effective management of beach access and use during the peak summer season:

- Eliminate traffic backups on both Maddox Boulevard and Beach Road by implementing a specified time pass system or other suitable system when beach parking space is filled.

- Continue private vehicle beach access as long as beach parking areas remain, and allow NPS to maintain the existing number of parking spaces (961) as long as the land base directly behind the dunes remain, realizing that this area will eventually be lost due to the natural movement of the barrier island. As natural forces reduce the land base capable of supporting the current parking, the number of spaces available will be reduced accordingly. As spaces are lost, an alternate means of transportation such as a shuttle system will need to be used.

- Encourage the establishment of a concessionaire, NPS, or Town operated shuttle transit system to provide beach access during the high use season.

- Coordinate with the NPS and Town of Chincoteague to identify a suitable off-site beach parking area to be used once the existing beach parking is lost.

- As a beach shuttle system is implemented, provide shuttle riders protection from hazardous weather conditions by allowing NPS to construct weather shelters for roughly 80 percent of peak shuttle capacity.

2. *Comprehensive Conservation Plan*

All national wildlife refuges are required to develop a CCP under the National Wildlife Refuge System Improvement Act of 1997. According to FWS, a CCP "describes the desired future conditions of a refuge or planning unit, provides long-range guidance and management direction to achieve the purposes of the refuge, helps fulfill the mission of the Refuge System, maintains and, where appropriate, restores the ecological integrity of each refuge and the Refuge System, helps achieve the goals of the National Wilderness Preservation System, and meets other mandates"[1]. In addition, the National Environmental Policy Act (NEPA) mandates that an environmental assessment or an environmental impact statement is developed within the CCP.

The pre-planning phase of the CNWR CCP, contracted separately to a third party by CNWR, proceeded concurrently with this transportation study; the report is not yet available. The transportation context of the CCP's planning alternatives, as understood from discussions with CNWR staff, is clear: options for managing and reconfiguring CNWR's public beach parking lots will be considered. The alternatives under consideration include the following actions relating to those parking lots:

- Retaining the lots as currently configured

- Relocating the lots and/or reducing their capacity

- Eliminating the lots entirely

---

[1] US Fish & Wildlife Service Refuge Planning: Northeast Region. What are CCP's?
http://www.fws.gov/northeast/planning/whatareccps html

The transportation alternatives developed later in this report correspond to the anticipated range of actions relative to the beach parking lots in the planning alternatives now under development in the CCP. Relevant parts of this study will be considered in the transportation element of the CCP.

3. *Transportation Assistance Group*

The TAG was conducted on behalf of the FWS and the NPS. The report documented observed site conditions, identified and analyzed transportation issues, and listed recommendations for action. The TAG team concluded that the important transportation issues arise from "peak visitation, limited parking facilities, and limited access", and states that: "There are multiple opportunities to improve the visitor experience, protect natural resources, and mitigate transportation challenges by undertaking a focused and targeted assessment of transportation alternatives".

Vehicular access to the beach parking lots by visitors, particularly on peak demand days, is at the heart of the congestion, parking, and impact issues identified by the TAG. The TAG's key recommendations for the transportation study were:

- Evaluate environmental and operational sustainability of transportation alternatives

- Evaluate how transportation solutions enhance wildlife values, improve access, and enhance visitor experience.

- Emphasize public-private partnership and public-public partnership opportunities

- Consider all possible transport modes in the development of the alternatives, including marine, vehicular, bicycle, and pedestrian modes

- Focus on the management and reduction of congestion through a variety of measures, including non-motorized and alternative transportation options, rather than on the elimination of vehicular access

- Complement primary data collection in the project area with several suggested peer site comparisons

- Solicit stakeholder feedback and engage the public in the development and evaluation of alternatives

- Evaluate impact of transportation alternatives on the area outside of CNWR, particularly in the Town of Chincoteague

4. *Assateague National Seashore General Management Plan (GMP)*

The preparation of the ASIS General Management Plan (GMP) is currently underway. According to the NPS Park Planning Program Standards (2004), the purpose of the GMP is "to ensure that park managers and stakeholders share a clearly defined understanding of the resource conditions, opportunities for visitor experience, and general kinds of management, access, and development that will best achieve the park's purpose and conserve its resources unimpaired for the enjoyment of future generations." The current ASIS GMP was completed in 1982, and ASIS, in coordination with the Northeast Region of NPS, has begun work on a new GMP that will guide management of ASIS for the next twenty years. To date, the process has focused on scoping and initial public outreach, with summer public outreach occurring in July and August 2009 and public meetings occurring in September 2009.

Approach

Project Overview and Methodology

The primary aims of this report are the following:

- Examines existing transportation conditions;

- Collects and analyzes relevant data, including input from the public;

- Assesses opportunities for partnerships with the co-applicants, and other stakeholders including local public agencies and businesses;

- Conducts a peer comparison study to identify best practices in the implementation of alternative transportation systems at similar sites; and

- Develops and evaluates transportation alternatives that may be considered for implementation by CNWR, its co-applicants, and other prospective partners.

The Volpe Center's execution of this project included the following tasks, which are briefly annotated to describe the methodology and flow of the work.

- Availability of Data and Resources
    - Literature search, including inquiries with the five ATPPL co-applicants
    - Web searches
    - Literature and data gathered during site visits

- Existing Conditions
    - Literature and data review
    - Site visits
    - Stakeholder interviews
    - Summary and analysis of existing conditions, including related plans and analyses

- Public Involvement Strategy and Outreach
    - Public meetings focused on area residents and stakeholders
    - Outreach to summer visitors at Pony Penning event, July 2009
    - Final public meeting to present findings
    - Website
    - Written comment solicitation via e-mail and postcards

- Partnership Assessment
    - Identification of existing and potential partners in consultation with CNWR
    - Assessment of potential partnership activities
    - Incorporation of partnerships into implementation of alternatives

- Peer Comparisons
    - Identification of peers in consultation with CNWR, ASIS, and Town
    - Development of discussion guide
    - Research and interviews
    - Selection of relevant sites for comparison
    - Assessments and "best practices" findings

- Alternatives Development and Analysis

o Development of list of interventions based on public input, existing conditions, previous plans, and consultation with CNWR
o Selection of relevant solutions
o Development of alternatives based on possible management scenarios
o Development and application of implementation factors
o Development and application of assessment criteria

Data Resources

Data resources used for the study consisted of data sets and reports and planning documents from consultants or government entities and interviews with the co-applicants and other relevant information sources. In addition, websites of local entities and newspaper articles from local media provided important local context and history. Primary sources of information included the following:

- CNWR and ASIS staff
- Town of Chincoteague staff and website
- Town of Chincoteague residents, business members, and visitors
- Accomack County and Accomack-Northampton Planning District Commission staff and websites
- Virginia Department of Transportation staff and website
- Virginia Department of Rail and Public Transportation staff and website
- *Chincoteague Beacon*
- Identified peers

2 Existing Conditions

This chapter characterizes general conditions and those relevant to transportation in the study area (Map 1), presents the supporting transportation-related data and information, and introduces the co-applicants and stakeholders. This information is, in part, the basis of the analysis recommendations made by the study.

The study area is located along the Eastern Shore of Virginia on the Delmarva Peninsula, the peninsula of land where Delaware, Maryland, and Virginia converge between the Chesapeake Bay and the Atlantic coastline (Map 1). It encompasses all of Chincoteague Island and the Virginia section of Assateague Island as well as part of Accomack County between Route 13 and the Atlantic Ocean and between the Maryland border and the southern edge of Chincoteague and Assateague Islands. Routes 13 and 175 are included because these roadways are the primary access routes to the Town of Chincoteague, CNWR, and ASIS. The study area also includes a National Aeronautics and Space Administration (NASA) facility, the Goddard Space Flight Center`s Wallops Flight Facility.

Map 1. Study Area.

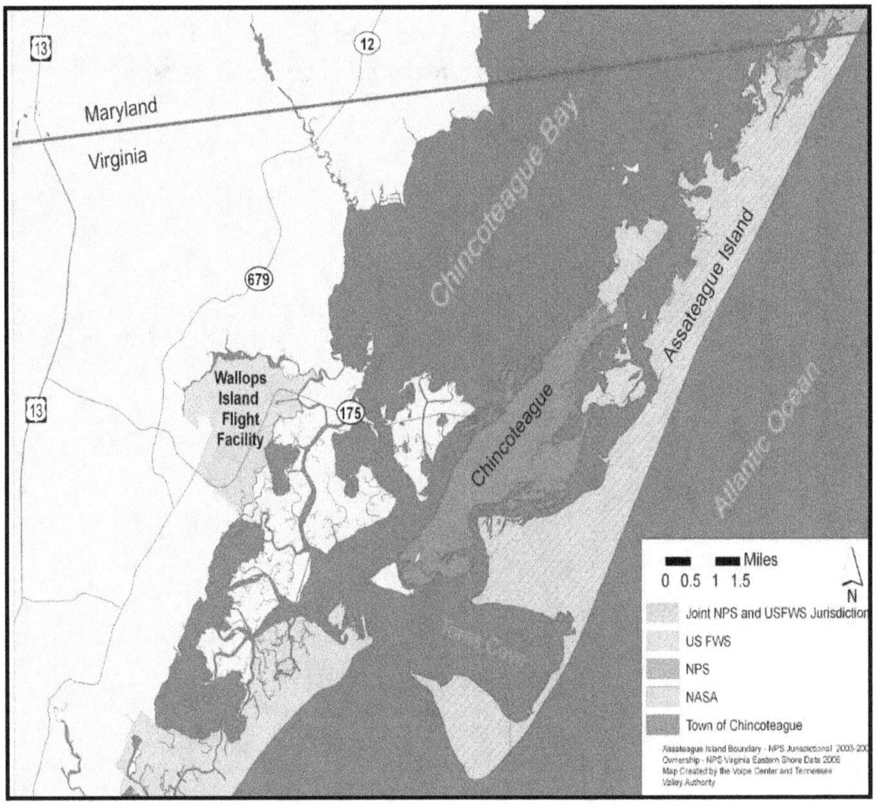

Source: ASIS, Tennessee Valley Authority, and Volpe Center staff using NPS and Virginia GIS data.

Project Co-Applicants

The application for funding for this planning project was jointly submitted by CNWR (FWS), ASIS (NPS), the Town of Chincoteague, Accomack County, and the Accomack-Northampton Planning District Commission (A-NPDC). The characteristics of each of the five co-applicants are important to understand in the context of this transportation planning study and will be discussed in this section.

Chincoteague National Wildlife Refuge (CNWR)

1. Overview

Most of the 14,000-acre CNWR (Map 2) is located on the Virginia portion of Assateague Island, a barrier beach island that extends over 30 miles along the Atlantic coast and is comprised of beach, dunes, fresh water swales, maritime forest, salt marsh and tidal mud flats. CNWR staff also manage three smaller islands that are located in the Virginia barrier islands chain: Assawoman Island (1,434 acres); Metompkin Island (174 acres); and Cedar Island (1,400 acres in fee title and 600 acres in easements). Additional CNWR lands are located on the north end of Chincoteague Island (546 acres at Wildcat Marsh) and on Morris Island (427 acres) which is located between Chincoteague and Assateague Islands.

Popular attractions within CNWR include the undeveloped, natural beach, the historic, functioning Assateague Lighthouse, and the Wildlife Loop and 6.5 miles of trails by which to view Chincoteague ponies, wildlife such as the sika elk, and migratory birds. The Herbert H. Bateman Educational and Administrative Center, a green facility that opened in 2003, is CNWR's visitor center and offers 5,000 square feet for interpretive natural history exhibits, educational programming, a 125 seat auditorium, and a classroom/wet lab.

2. Management

CNWR was established in 1943 under the authority of the Migratory Bird Conservation Act as a sanctuary for migratory and wintering waterfowl. It has since been designated as a Globally Important Bird Area by the American Bird Conservancy, a key location along a top birding trail by the National Audubon Society, and a Site of International Importance within the Western Hemisphere Shorebird Reserve Network, a conservation partnership of stewards and landowners led by the Manomet Center for Conservation Sciences.

CNWR is part of the National Wildlife Refuge System – a system of public lands set aside for habitat and wildlife conservation. The refuge system is made up of more than 150 million acres of land on over 550 national wildlife refuges and has a goal of maintaining "the biological integrity, diversity and environmental health of these natural resources for the benefit of present and future generations." While conservation and management of wildlife and its habitats are the main objectives of the refuge system, FWS also maintains six wildlife-dependent uses when appropriate: hunting, fishing, wildlife observation, wildlife photography, environmental education and interpretation.[2] FWS manages CNWR to protect and conserve the diversity of native species and habitats located within its lands and waters. Specifically important is the critical habitat for migratory waterfowl and shorebirds.

---

[2] U.S. Fish and Wildlife Service. National Refuge System Website. 2009. http://www.fws.gov/refuges/

Map 2. Chincoteague National Wildlife Refuge and Town of Chincoteague.

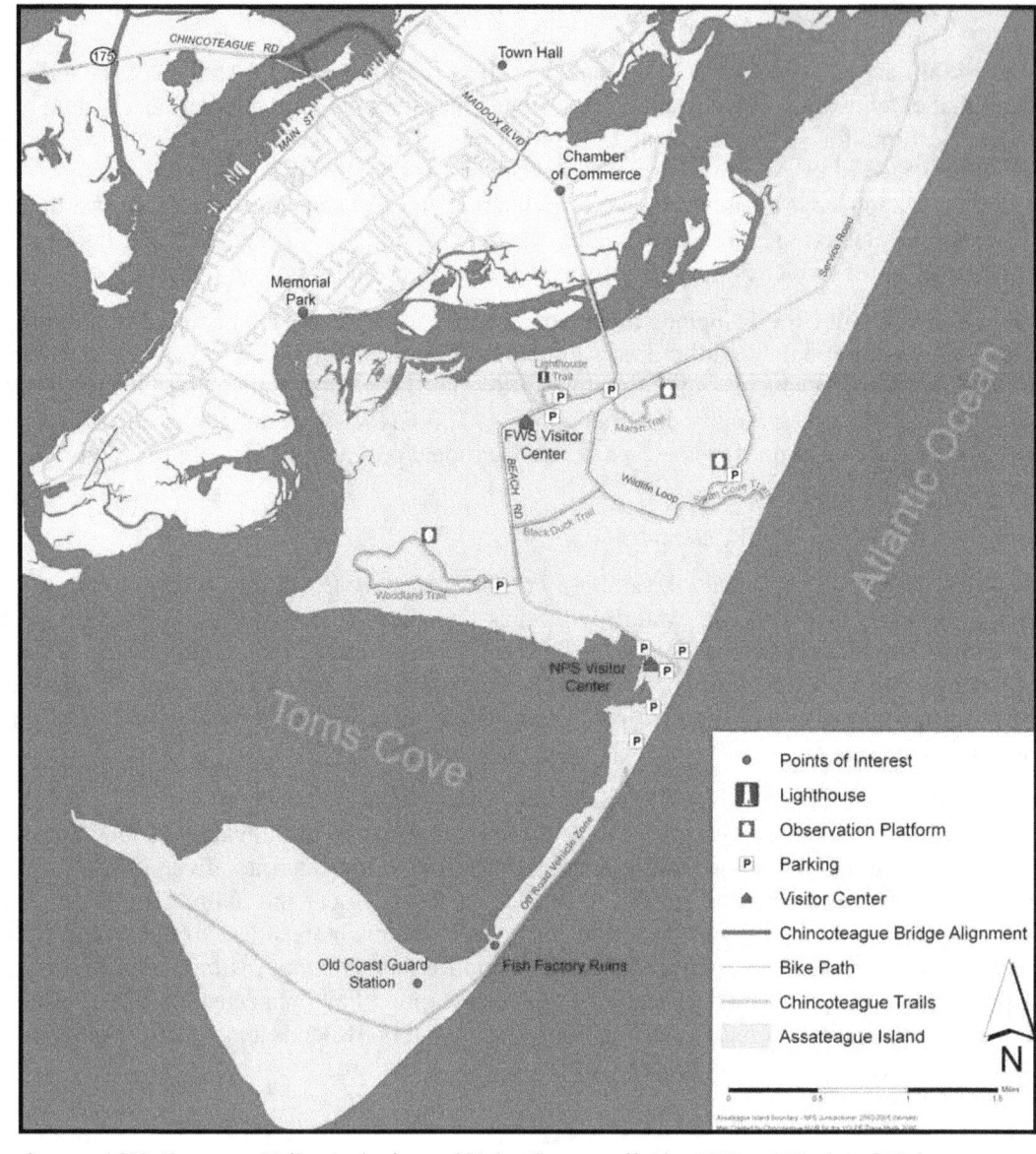

Source: ASIS, Tennessee Valley Authority, and Volpe Center staff using NPS and Virginia GIS data.

CNWR's main environmental management tasks support the conservation and protection of threatened and endangered species such as the Piping Plover, Delmarva Peninsula fox squirrel, loggerhead turtle, and sea beach amaranth, and of the habitat that supports hundreds of other species of flora and fauna. To accomplish these tasks, CNWR closes certain beach areas during the piping plover nesting season and manipulates water levels in moist soil management units that cover 2,600 acres. In addition, CNWR allows the famous Chincoteague ponies to graze in two areas of CNWR through a special use permit with the owners, the Chincoteague Volunteer Fire Company.

According to the CNWR *Master Plan*, recreational use and related development on Assateague Island were originally authorized by Congress in 1957, including the provision for construction for a bridge and road to CNWR as well as for recreational facilities on the southeastern shore of the island. Under special agreement with the FWS, the Chincoteague-Assateague Bridge and Beach Authority, a political subdivision of the Commonwealth of Virginia, developed and managed beachfront recreational facilities and visitor services. The 1957 law also authorized several other development projects, namely overnight accommodations and a highway running the length of Assateague Island, but controversy surrounding environmental, administrative, and fiscal aspects of the plans led to their eventual elimination as requirements in a 1976 Master Plan amendment.

CNWR now faces the prospect of major long-term physical environmental changes along the shoreline that could adversely affect the public beach and its adjacent parking lots. Discussion of this issue appears in the Assateague Island National Seashore section (2.a) and elsewhere in the report.

3. *Visitation*

The geographical and jurisdictional relationship between the CNWR and the Virginia District of ASIS and the nature of the data available mean that visitation to one is considered visitation to the other. CNWR and the Virginia District of ASIS attract over 1.2 million visits per year. This number has been fairly stable for the past 30 years. According to FWS, CNWR is one of the most visited refuges in the nation.[3] Visitation data are collected by NPS for all units and subunits. Visits to the Virginia District of ASIS are calculated based on data from an FWS traffic counter located on the exit lane by the fee booths on Beach Road.[4] Figures 3 and 4 provide detailed information on visitation by year and month.

Peak visitation (250-300,000 per month) occurs during the summer, in July and August, primarily due to the beach-going visitors, but CNWR and ASIS also attract many birders, naturalists, and other tourists during the spring and fall.[5] According to a 2006 economic impact report by FWS, non-Virginia residents accounted for 89 percent of visits to CNWR.[6]

Figure 3. Number of Visits to CNWR and the Virginia District of ASIS 1967-2008[7]

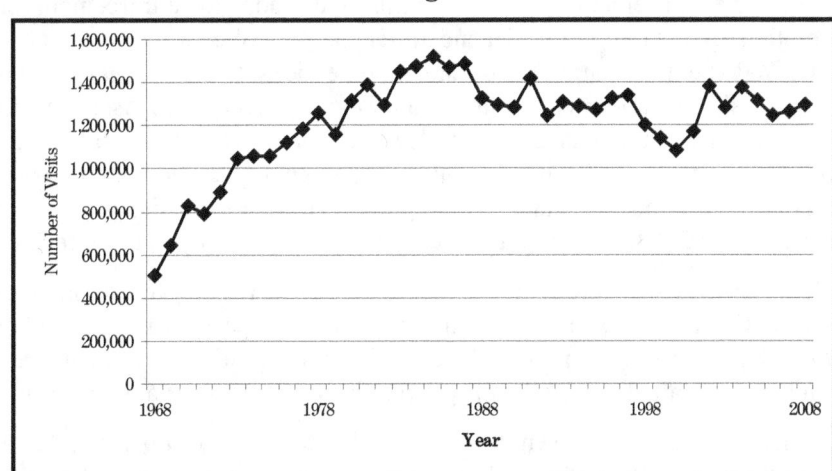

Source: ASIS/NPS data, compiled by the Volpe Center.

---

[3] Chincoteague National Wildlife Refuge. www.fws.gov/refuges/profiles/index.cfm?id=51570

[4] The total number of vehicles is reduced for buses (actual count), non-recreation vehicles (150 per month), and non-reportable vehicles (estimated by season) and then multiplied by a people per vehicle multiplier of 3.2 (this number has varied throughout the years). Finally, the number of bus visitors to the district (bus count multiplied by 45) and the number of visitors arriving on the beach by a boat concessioner is added. The boat visitor count was added in 2007; before 1998, a count for pedestrians and bicyclists reported by FWS and NPS staff was also included but now is not.

[5] NPS Stats: ASIS YTD Report (http://www nature nps.gov/stats)

[6] Banking on Nature 2006: The Economic Benefits to Local Communities of National Wildlife Visitation. September 2007. Division of Economics, U.S. Fish and Wildlife Service.

[7] (1968-1985) Analysis of Traffic Management Options. June 1986. Barry Lawson Associates, Inc.; (1986-2001) ASIS records; (2002-2008) National Park Service Public Use Statistics Office.

Figure 4. Number of Visits to CNWR and Virginia District of ASIS by Month 2006-2008

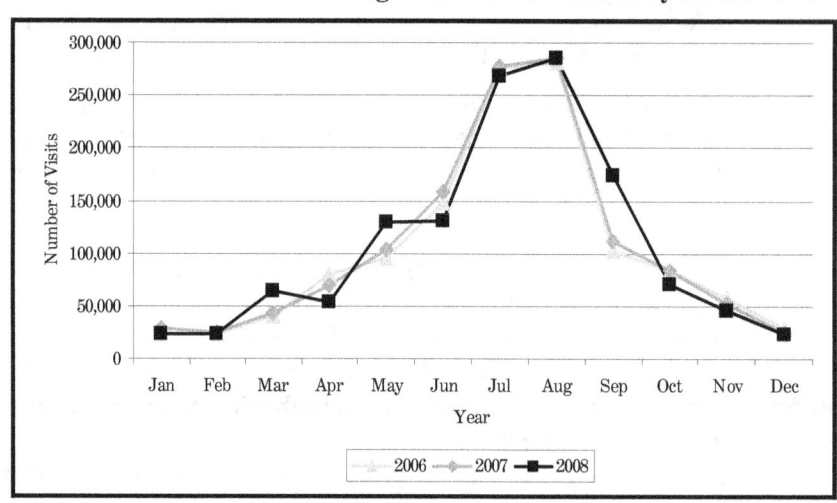

Source: ASIS/NPS data, compiled by the Volpe Center.

4. Entrance and Recreation Fees

Entrance and recreation fees provide a vital source of revenue for improving facilities and services for visitors to CNWR. CNWR receives 80 percent of the fees it collects and uses them for visitor services projects, maintenance and enhancement of facilities, trails, and roads, law enforcement related to visitor safety, habitat restoration related to wildlife-dependent recreation, collection costs and operations. For example, in 2007, CNWR spent recreation fee dollars on bike racks, two emergency call boxes, interpretive signs and kiosks, visitor services interns, a temporary Recreation Assistant, refuge brochures for visitor orientation, bike trail maintenance, fee collection operations, visitor health and safety services, and family activities for special events. The remaining 20 percent of fees collected goes to the FWS Northeast Regional Office (Region 5) to fund a small grants program for visitor services projects at other refuges within the region. In 2008, CNWR retained approximately $700,000 of its revenues.

CNWR implemented a new fee structure in 2008, consisting of a new daily fee, an increase to the weekly entrance fee, and the addition of an expanded amenity fee for beach parking for the CNWR annual pass and the Federal Duck Stamp program. In 2010, the daily fee will be increased. (2.d addresses these changes in detail and more detailed ASIS/CNWR parking information and data appear in Appendix B).

Entrance fees are collected year-round seven days a week, but the hours of operation for the entrance fee booth (Figure 5) vary throughout the year; Table 1 shows the schedule. Credit card machines were added to the fee booths in 2007. When the fee booths are unstaffed, the honor system is used. Visitors are expected to use the iron ranger, a self-serve pay station, which is located outside the CNWR visitor center. Visitors can pay the $5.00 daily fee by taking an envelope, inserting $5.00, and dropping the envelope into the vaulted iron ranger. CNWR is working on plans to install off-site pass purchase machines and recently received $350,000 in funding from the Paul S. Sarbanes Transit in the Parks Program to provide Intelligent Information Traffic Systems, which may include fee collection systems.

Figure 5. CNWR Entrance Booths.

Source: CNWR website (USFWS). http://www.fws.gov/northeast/chinco/fees.html.

Table 1. CNWR Fee Booth Hours of Operation.

Dates	Days	Hours
January 1 - March 31	Saturday and Sunday	8:00am - 4:00pm
April 1 - May 24	Daily	8:00am – 4:00pm
May 25-September 2	Daily	8:00am – 8:00pm (weekends 7am-8pm)
September 3 - October 31	Daily	8:00am – 4:00pm (weekends 8am-5pm)
November 1 - December 31	Saturday and Sunday	8:00am - 4:00pm

Source: CNWR.

Assateague Island National Seashore

1. Overview

ASIS was created in 1965 to preserve Assateague Island's unique Mid-Atlantic coastal resources and natural ecosystem conditions and processes while providing high quality resource-compatible recreational opportunities. ASIS encompasses all of Assateague Island and most of the smaller islands immediately adjacent to it. ASIS also has administrative responsibilities for the water column surrounding Assateague Island. This administrative boundary extends one-half mile out into the Atlantic Ocean and into the back bays and mid-channel waters on the western edge of the island and half the distance to other islands or the mainland.

ASIS headquarters and main visitor center are located on the mainland at the Maryland point of access to Assateague Island. However, they also maintain a visitor information and ranger station in Virginia.

2. Management

According to the CNWR *Master Plan*, the Assateague Island Seashore Act (1965) established ASIS and provided that NPS could administer ASIS:

> "for general purposes of public outdoor recreation with the qualification that land and water within the refuge be administered for purposes under laws and regulations applicable to national wildlife refuges,

including administration for public recreation use in accordance with the provisions of the Refuge Recreation Act"

In addition, the Act authorized the Department of Interior to acquire all of the rights, title, and property of the Chincoteague-Assateague Bridge and Beach Authority. Acquisition was completed in 1966 by NPS and NPS continues to own and manage the bridge between Chincoteague and Assateague as well as the public road from the NPS Visitor Center to the public beach.

Since the Act, ASIS has managed public use of the Toms Cove beach as an agent of FWS. These activities were clarified in a 1990 Interagency Agreement between FWS and NPS. Under the agreement, ASIS administers public activities on a five-mile portion of beach and operates a visitor recreation program. Within this area, ASIS maintains a visitor center, lifeguard-protected swimming beach, restrooms, bathhouses, parking areas, pedestrian trails and coordinates an over-sand vehicle area.

3. Shoreline change

CNWR and ASIS face the prospect of major long-term physical environmental changes along the shoreline that could adversely affect the public beach and its adjacent parking lots as well as other key infrastructure. This is a natural phenomenon that is increasingly being exacerbated by severe storm events (the most recent example of which was Nor'easter Ida in November 2009) and climate change, which will be addressed further in Chapter 3.

ASIS staff have developed a number of maps that show the historic shoreline changes on Assateague Island. Map 3 is a time series that shows the changes in Toms Cove from 1850 to 2005. The southern end of Assateague Island is moving westward and Toms Cove Hook is increasing in land mass as the connection between the Hook and the rest of the Island is shrinking. These maps do not yet capture the impact of the November 2009 storm, which altered the landscape and shape of the Island significantly, including the near-detachment of the Hook from the rest of the Island.

Previously, there had been dune maintenance and restoration efforts in this portion of Assateague Island, but these activities were stopped once it was determined that they actually interfere with natural processes that would the island to rebuild itself to the west.

These landform changes clearly demonstrate the threat of storm damage to the parking lots and beaches, a threat that is likely to grow with the rise in sea level and increased frequency and intensity of storms predicted as a result of climate change.

Map 3. Shoreline Change for Toms Cove, Assateague Island, from 1850 to 2005.

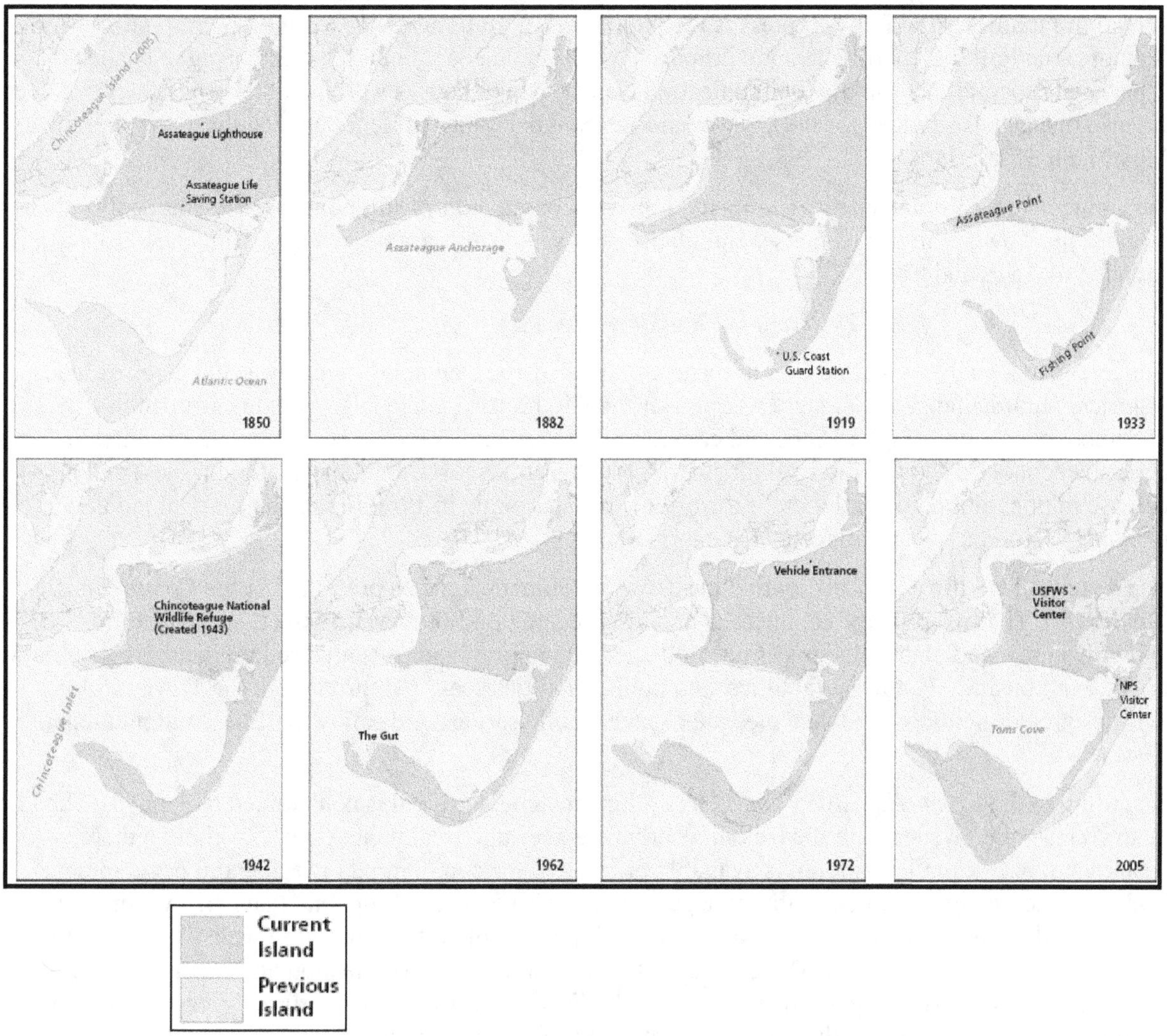

Source: ASIS/NPS.

Town of Chincoteague

Chincoteague's small size, relatively high population density, significant increase in population during the summer season, and its unique reliance on the tourism industry, are important factors in considering its transportation network and access to CNWR. In addition, Chincoteague's future development is limited by the island's physical geography, historic properties and character, and the presence of protected Federal lands, which contribute to the seasonal traffic congestion and may also restrict some congestion mitigation measures such as roadway widening.

1. Overview

The Town of Chincoteague was incorporated in 1908 and subsequently annexed land on three different occasions, most recently in 1989. Currently, the entire Island is part of the Town of Chincoteague. The Town has a mayor-town council form of government that includes six council members. The Town Manager is the chief administrative officer in Chincoteague and serves as clerk to the Town Council.

The Town has several departments as well as several boards and committees that oversee specific Town functions and assets. The Planning Commission administers the Town plan and promotes the health, safety and general welfare of the Town. The Recreation and Community Enhancement Committee is responsible for the Town bicycle plan and overseeing the management, maintenance and construction of recreation facilities. The Pony Express is the public transportation service for the Town. The Town of Chincoteague Police Department is the primary law enforcement agency for Chincoteague Island. The Department operates a 24-hour Communication Center, which houses 911 and other emergency services, and also dispatches services for the CNWR and ASIS under an agreement between the Town and the Department of Interior.

The Chincoteague Volunteer Fire Company, Inc is a separate non-profit, non-governmental entity that provides the Town with fire response, ambulance, and search and rescue services, which are also extended to ASIS and CNWR.

2. *Land use and development*

Chincoteague Island was settled by European colonists in 1671 on approximately 1,500 acres of land. Historical records indicate that there were fewer than 40 houses on the island in the early 1800s. Steamboat connections in the 1800s and completion of the Route 175 Causeway in 1922 resulted in increased economic activity in certain industries (such as the aquaculture and seafood trades) and an increase in population. Completion of the bridge to Assateague in 1962 fueled the tourism industry, replacing seafood trade as Chincoteague's top industry.

Map 4 shows land use as of 2005 within the Town of Chincoteague as presented in the *Comprehensive Plan* (2009). The two primary commercial areas are located on South Main Street, in the historic downtown area, and along Maddox Boulevard. The remaining land uses are predominantly residential or vacant, with businesses, tourist facilities, and public facilities scattered throughout the Town. Public facilities include schools, the Chincoteague Center, public service and safety facilities, and municipal offices.

According to the *Comprehensive Plan* (2009), Chincoteague's growth is constrained by land, capacity of the drinking water system, and the lack of a centralized sewage treatment system. Although there is vacant land, only a limited amount is available or feasible for commercial or residential development. For drinking water, Chincoteague is entirely dependent upon five miles of pipeline that carry water from underground wells on the mainland to the island; withdrawal of water from these wells is regulated by the Virginia Department of Health. There is currently no central sewage collection and treatment system serving the Island. Instead, wastewater is primarily disposed of by discharge directly into seepage pits, cesspools, or by the use of holding tanks or septic tanks and drain fields. Some residents have recently installed "package" sewage treatment systems. A municipal wastewater treatment system would allow for an increase in year-round housing units.

3. *Demographics*

The total year-round population in Chincoteague is approximately 4,300. However, many Chincoteague residents do not live on the island full-time and many visitors to Chincoteague rent places to stay for extended periods of time. The *Comprehensive Plan* (2009) estimates that the summer population for Chincoteague increases to 15,000. Most hotels, motels, and bed and breakfast establishments are located along Main Street and Maddox Boulevard; rental houses and apartments are located throughout the Town. Map 5 displays areas in which seasonally vacant housing is concentrated, notably in the northern part of Chincoteague Island and west of Maddox Boulevard as the road approaches the bridge to CNWR. The *Comprehensive Plan* (2009) also notes that high peak season occupancy rates indicate that additional overnight accommodations would be necessary to increase the number of overnight visitors to the Island.

Although the current median age in Chincoteague (46 years) is significantly higher than those of Accomack County (39) and the State (37), and state and national trends indicate increasing senior populations, the Chincoteague *Comprehensive Plan* (2009) projects that all age groups will increase equally due to the employment growth, especially at the NASA Wallops Island facility.

Map 4. Town of Chincoteague: Existing Land Use (2005).

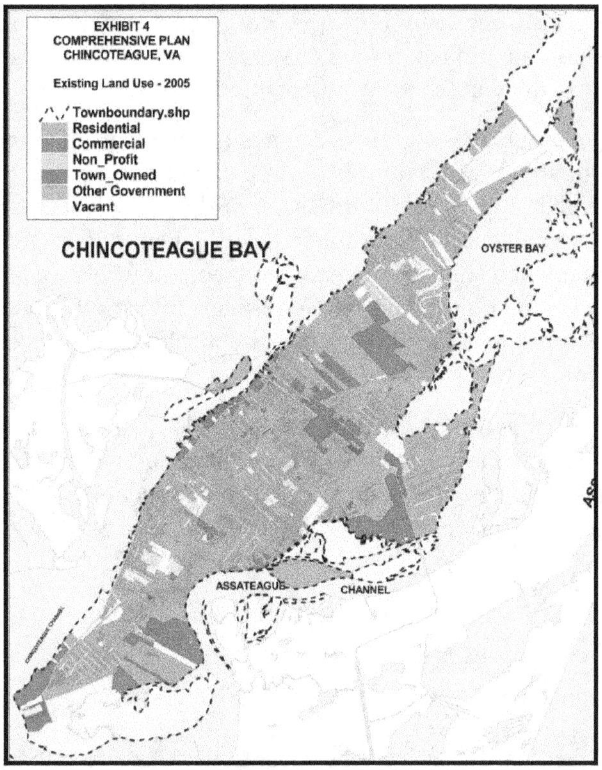

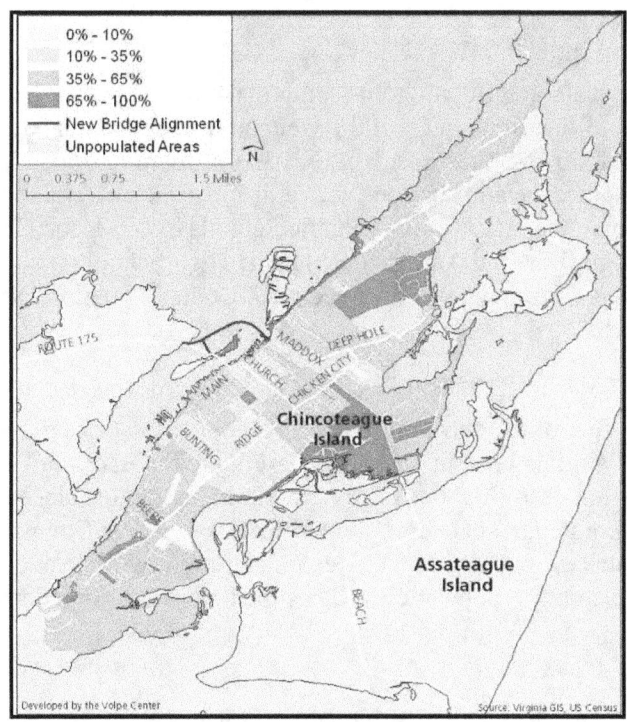

Source: *Comprehensive Plan*, Town of Chincoteague, 2009.

Map 5. Chincoteague Seasonally-Vacant Housing.

Source: Volpe Center, using U.S. Census (2000) data.

4. Economic characteristics

The Town of Chincoteague's local economy is closely linked to the tourism and recreational activities that take place at CNWR. Thus, any transportation changes and improvements that may impact visitor access and enjoyment are of particular economic interest to the Town.

According to the 2000 U.S. Census, the largest percentage (20 percent) of Chincoteague's workers are employed in tourism and tourism-related industries, while another 16 percent is employed in retail, which is dominated by tourist-oriented shops. The Town's *Comprehensive Plan* clearly states that proximity to ASIS and CNWR continues to be its largest economic development opportunity. In 2006, the FWS Division of Economics carried out a study of the economic benefit of National Wildlife Refuges on their local areas, with a detailed examination of 80 specific refuges, including Chincoteague. The report's validity has been questioned but it concluded that visitors contributed significant expenditures and tax revenue to the Town and County. [8]

As mentioned above, a variety of accommodations are available in the Town, including over 20 hotels or motels, about a dozen bed and breakfast establishments, and numerous rental homes, cottages, efficiencies, and apartments. There are four campgrounds on Chincoteague, all of which report 70 percent to 80 percent occupancy from June through Labor Day[9] including:

1. Maddox - 339 hook-ups and 250 tent sites
2. Toms Cove - 914 camp sites and 24 mobile home sites
3. Inlet View - 300 sites, 4 cottages and 5 mobile homes
4. Pine Grove - 150 campsites.

The presence of the NASA facility and adjacent business activity is also important to the economy of the Town and Accomack County.

Accomack County

1. Overview

Accomack County and Northampton County to its south make up Virginia's Eastern Shore, a 70-mile long, 15-mile wide portion of the southern tip of the Delmarva Peninsula. The area is predominantly farmland, marshes, and small towns. Accomack County has a Board of Supervisors, one member of which is a resident of Chincoteague and has been active in supporting efforts to identify transportation issues and explore solutions. Accomack County Public Schools oversees the Chincoteague Elementary School (kindergarten through fifth grade) and Chincoteague High School (sixth through twelfth grade). The County is also part of the Northampton and Accomack County Planning District, another co-applicant described below.

2. Demographics

Accomack County is the larger of the two counties, with a population of nearly 40,000, or 75 percent of the total population of the Virginia Eastern Shore. According to the *Accomack Comprehensive Plan* (2008), Accomack County has seen slow but steady growth in population since 1970. Based on 2000 Census data, the Virginia Employment Commission projects Accomack County's population to grow 21 percent by 2030, or an annual growth rate of 0.65 percent. Within Accomack County, Chincoteague makes up 10 percent of the county's population and has the highest housing density in the county.

---

[8] Division of Economics, U.S. Fish and Wildlife Service, "Banking on Nature 2006: The Economic Benefits to Local Communities of National Wildlife Visitation", September 2007.

[9] Chesapeake Bay Bridge-Tunnel Toll Impact Study, October 2001.

3. Economic characteristics

The *Accomack County Comprehensive Plan* (2008)[10], relying on data from the Accomack County and Northampton County Commissioners of Revenue and the Chincoteague Chamber of Commerce, reports that in 2000 about 83 percent of Accomack County's tourist-related tax revenue was generated by the activities and amenities that the Town of Chincoteague, CNWR, and ASIS provide visitors.

According to the Town of Chincoteague's *Comprehensive Plan* (2009), in response to the existing activities as well as the potential for additional growth at and around the NASA facility, Accomack County has created a task force to focus on the development of a business park and learning center. The task force has identified a site just outside the Wallops Island facility main gate and a preliminary engineering report, phase one environmental review, and development plan have been completed. The proposed Wallops Research Park would be co-owned by four entities: Accomack County; NASA; the Marine Science Consortium; and the United States Navy.

Accomack-Northampton Planning District Commission

1. Overview

The Accomack-Northampton Planning District Commission (A-NPDC) is the Virginia Eastern Shore's regional planning agency. Its jurisdiction consists of Accomack County and Northampton County, including 19 incorporated towns. It has a Board of Commissioners and a staff of 15 in its planning, housing production, and housing services departments. A-NPDC works on a number of initiatives related to meeting Federal and State planning requirements, such as the US Economic Development Administration's Comprehensive Economic Development Strategy (CEDS) requirement for economic development district designation and the Virginia Department of Transportation's requirement of an adopted bicycle facilities plan in order to receive project funding for bicycle facilities.

2. Transportation planning studies and initiatives

A-NPDC staff have led or participated in a number of planning studies and initiatives relevant to the study area. A-NPDC participated in the Project Management Team for the *Route 13/Wallops Island Access Management Study*. In addition, A-NPDC staff have been working on public access improvements (floating docks) to the Seaside Water Trail with the Virginia Department of Environmental Quality since 2003. A-NPDC has also actively worked with the Eastern Shore of Virginia National Wildlife Refuge and Northampton County to construct a 2.5 paved bicycle path along a former railroad right-of-way from the Refuge to the entrance of Kiptopeke State Park, at the intersection of Cedar Grove Drive (Route 645) and Route 13; a pre-solicitation for construction bids was posted in July 2009.

Stakeholders

There are several other stakeholder groups with interest in the study area and, in particular, local transportation issues. These include both operators of existing transportation systems and potential future partners for the planning and implementing of transportation solutions.

Town of Chincoteague - Pony Express

The Pony Express is the public transit service owned and operated by the Town of Chincoteague. The trolley was recommended in the *Chincoteague 2020 Transportation Plan* (2002); it began operating in 2004 with Demonstration Project Grant funding from the Virginia Department of Rail and Public

---

[10] "Respecting the Past, Creating the Future: Accomack County Comprehensive Plan", May 14, 2008, http://www.co.accomack.va.us/Planning/2008_comprehensive_plan_update.html.

Transportation (DRPT) and a contribution from the Town.[11] Since then, funding for operations has evolved to include a mix of Federal (FTA Section 5311 grant), State (DRPT assistance programs), and Town funds, as well as operating revenues (fares and advertising). Figure 6 shows funding data and sources from FY03 to FY09.

Figure 6. Operating Funding for Chincoteague Trolley FY03-FY09.

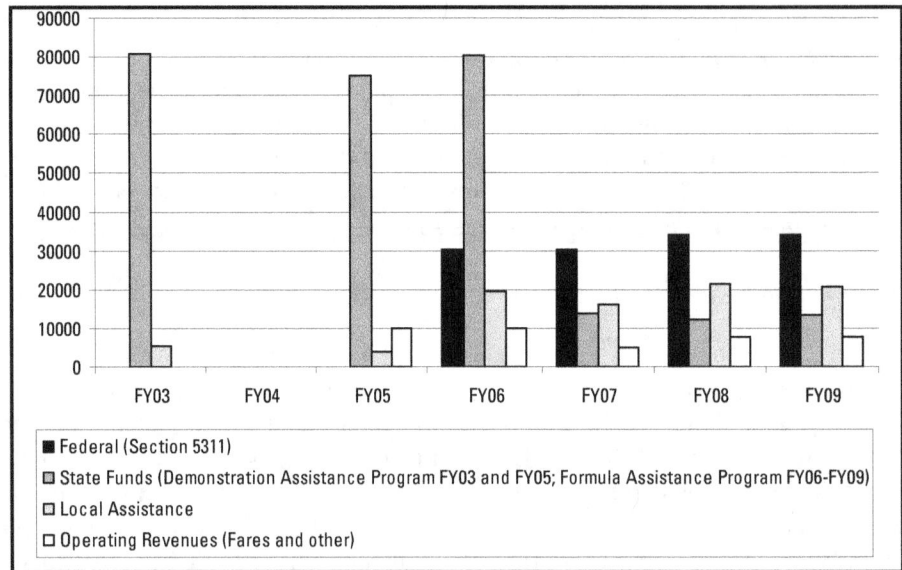

Source: Virginia Department of Rail and Public Transportation, DRPT Six-Year Improvement Plans. http://www.drpt.virginia.gov/about/finance.aspx.

The highlights of the fleet acquisition history are as follows:

- **2004** – Town funded leasing of a trolley.
- **2005** – Town acquired a used trolley from the neighboring town of Greenbackville.[12] Non-compliance with ADA accessibility standards prompted the Town to lease a special shuttle to accommodate disabled passengers.
- **2006** – Town bought two new trolleys, with wheelchair lifts and racks for paid advertisements, funded primarily by the Federal Surface Transportation Program, with contributions from the State and the Town.[13][14]
- **2007** – Town Council authorized up to $10,000 for the purchase of a used trolley to replace an older trolley.[15] This proposal is in the DRPT's *FY09 Six-Year Improvement Plan* and is scheduled for FY13.[16]

---

[11] Virginia Department of Rail and Public Transportation. FY2003 Public Transportation Improvement Program. http://www.drpt.virginia.gov/studies/files/DRPT-FY03-ProgramOfProjects.pdf

12 Furness, Stephen. Chincoteague Beacon. December 9, 2004.

[13] Virginia Department of Rail and Public Transportation. FY 2006 Rail and Public Transportation Improvement Program. http://www.drpt.virginia.gov/studies/files/DRPT-FY06-ProgramOfProjects.pdf

[14] Furness, Stephen. Chincoteague Beacon. November 3, 2005.

[15] November 5, 2007 Town Council Meeting

http://www.chincoteaguereports.com/my_weblog/chincoteague-town-council/page/2/

[16] Virginia Department of Rail and Public Transportation. FY 2006 Rail and Public Transportation Improvement Program. http://www.drpt.virginia.gov/about/files/FY09%20DRPT%20SYP-Revised%20Final.pdf

NASA

NASA operates the Goddard Space Flight Center's Wallops Flight Facility, located off of Route 175 between Route 13 and the Chincoteague Causeway (Map 6). It was established in 1945 by the National Advisory Committee for Aeronautics as a center for aeronautic research. It has launched approximately 16,000 rockets and expects an increase in commercial launch activity in the near future.

The Flight Center employs 750 Federal employees and contractors but also shares the space with both the United States Navy's Surface Combat Systems Center, which employs 300 people, and the National Oceanic and Atmospheric Administration Command and Data Acquisition Station, which employs 100 people.[17]

The site is also home to the Mid-Atlantic Regional Spaceport (MARS), which offers launch facilities for government, commercial, and academic/scientific uses. In December 2008, NASA selected Orbital Sciences Corporation, a space technology company based in Northern Virginia, to perform cargo transportation services to the International Space Station once the space shuttle program ends in 2010. Orbital has announced its intention to use MARS as one of its main launch sites.[18]

NASA's facilities include a visitor center that is open 10 am – 4 pm daily between July 4 and Labor Day[19] and currently receives approximately 50,000 to 60,000 visitors annually.[20] The visitor center contains a paved parking lot, and overflow parking is available in a nearby field. The visitor facility has never closed due to lack of parking. Visitation to the facility spikes during events such as rocket launches. The Chincoteague *Comprehensive Plan* (2009) reported that NASA is considering expanding the visitor center.

Virginia Department of Transportation and Other State Agencies

The Virginia Department of Transportation (VDOT) is the state agency responsible for building, maintaining and operating the State's roads, bridges and tunnels, including all important roads in the study area. VDOT is now managing the construction of the new Route 175 bridge that connects the Causeway to Chincoteague Island (project detail in 2.c).

VDOT collects and analyzes traffic data and conducts planning studies, such as the Route 13/Wallops Island Access Management Study. VDOT also manages a traffic and traveler information website, www.511va.org, which provides road condition information, including feeds from traffic cameras that VDOT owns and operates. However, these services do not yet cover the Eastern Shore. The website does have links to the Chincoteague Pony Express website.

The Town of Chincoteague lies within the Hampton Roads District, which has a Traffic Operations Center, and the nearest VDOT Residency Office is located in Accomack, 30 miles south of Chincoteague.

---

[17] Chincoteague Comprehensive Plan (2009).

[18] Orbital Selected by NASA For $1.9 Billion Space Station Cargo Delivery Contract. Orbital Press Release, 23 December 2008. http://www.orbital.com/NewsInfo/release.asp?prid=680

[19] Open 10am-4pm Thursday through Monday from March to June and from September to November, and 10am-4pm Monday through Friday from December to February.

[20] Chincoteague Comprehensive Plan (2009).

Map 6. NASA's Wallops Flight Facility in Relation to the Town of Chincoteague and CNWR.

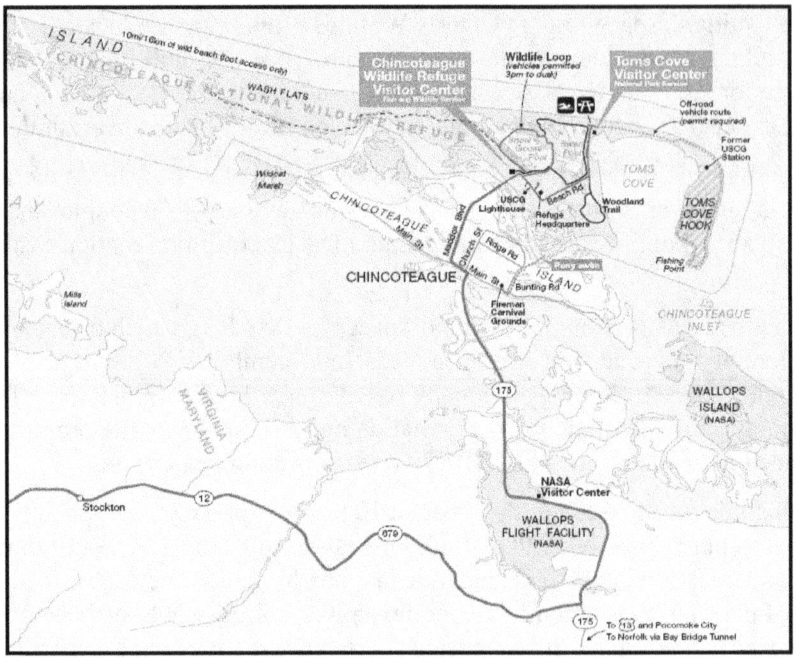

Source: ASIS/NPS.

There are several other state agencies that are involved in transportation. The Department of Motor Vehicles, for example, collects safety information, such as crash statistics. The DRPT, mentioned above as a main funding source for Pony Express, oversees rail, public transportation, and commuter services and aims to improve the mobility of people and goods and to expand transportation choices. The Department of Environmental Quality is home to the Virginia Coastal Zone Management Program, which oversees the Seaside Water Trail, a kayak and canoe trail along the Eastern Shore. Finally, the Department of Emergency Management oversees emergency and disaster planning functions statewide, such as evacuation planning and emergency response.

STAR Transit

Shore Transit and Rideshare (STAR) Transit is the public transportation provider for A-NPDC. Service began in 1996 with a grant from the DRPT. STAR Transit currently runs four fixed routes on weekdays, one of which serves the Town of Chincoteague and will be described below, and a demand-response service. It also offers a deviated route service (1.5 miles) on all its routes for those with an approved ADA application. STAR Transit buses are all equipped with external bicycle racks.[21]

According to the *2008 Accomack-Northampton Mobility Plan*, STAR Transit has an annual ridership of 39,000 and utilizes eleven 12-, 15-, and 20-passenger vans, nine of which are handicap-accessible (see Figure 7). None of these vehicles are used on the weekends. STAR Transit is required by the counties to provide vehicles for any evacuation activities that occur.

---

[21] STAR Transit website. www.mystartransit.com

Figure 7. STAR Transit Vehicle.

Source: STAR Transit website and brochure. www.mystartransit.com.

Chincoteague Natural History Association

Chincoteague's full-time and seasonal residents are active in their neighborhoods and in associations that serve the public interest. The Chincoteague Natural History Association (CNHA) is one group that has a strong stake in the continued popularity of, and access to, CNWR.

The CNHA is a non-profit association established in partnership with the U.S. Fish and Wildlife Service. The purpose of the CNHA is to promote a better understanding and appreciation of CNWR, the Eastern Shore of Virginia National Wildlife Refuge, and the natural history and environment of Virginia's Eastern Shore in general. The CNHA produces and provides interpretive and educational material for refuge visitors and for local teachers, funds student interns, and enables both refuges to receive matching grants for workshops and programs. Proceeds from memberships and items sold at the retail store at the CNWR Visitor Center are used to support and enhance the interpretive programs, projects, and activities at both of the refuges. The CHNA owns and operates a small tour bus, which they use to provide interpretive tours of CNWR.

A similar organization, the Assateague Island Alliance, is a new non-profit association, established on January 1, 2008, which serves as the dedicated friends group, or cooperating association, for ASIS. Its goal is to work in partnership with ASIS to advance the scientific, educational, interpretive, preservation, recreational, and management objectives of ASIS.

Chincoteague Chamber of Commerce and Other Business Associations

The Chincoteague Chamber of Commerce is a non-profit, volunteer membership organization that serves as the leading representative for the businesses on Chincoteague Island. It was founded in 1954 by a group of businessmen and as of 2007 had 272 members. Most of the member businesses are tourism-related, including hotels and campgrounds, restaurants, and retail such as bicycle rental places. Consequently, the Chamber is focused on promoting the tourism industry. The Chamber distributes a visitor guide at Virginia Welcome Centers and other sites year-round as well as in response to requests by mail or telephone. The Chamber's office is located inside the large rotary on Maddox Boulevard (Figure 8). The Chamber participates as a member in the U.S. Chamber of Commerce, the Virginia Chamber of Commerce, the Eastern Shore Chamber of Commerce, the Eastern Shore Tourism Commission, and the Virginia Tourism Commission.

Figure 8. Chincoteague Chamber of Commerce.

Source: Volpe Center, photograph, July 2009.

There are three other business associations within the Town of Chincoteague. The Chincoteague Island Charter Boat Association is a non-profit organization that serves 29 local charter boat companies. The Historic Main Street Merchants Association consists of 42 specialty shops, restaurants, bed and breakfasts, and vacation rental businesses located along Main Street in Chincoteague. The Chincoteague Cultural Alliance is a non-profit organization focused on promoting arts and culture on Chincoteague Island and the Eastern Shore. Its members consist mainly of gallery owners and artists and it focuses mainly on holding a variety of events and festivals.

Current Transportation Conditions

This section describes the transportation conditions, characteristics, and services for Chincoteague and Assateague Islands. Subsections include automobile traffic and circulation, traffic safety, parking, transit, cycling and pedestrian activity, and marine transportation. This information is essential to identifying transportation problems and solutions.

Automobile Traffic and Circulation

Private automobile travel is the most popular mode of transportation in the region. Vehicles travel via U.S. Route 13 on the mainland to Route 175, the only access road to Chincoteague Island and to the Virginia section of Assateague Island. Travel on the islands is serviced primarily by two-lane local roads. VDOT owns, maintains and manages most roadways in the State, including all roadways in the Town of Chincoteague.

1. Regional corridors

U.S. Route 13 is the principal north-south corridor linking the Eastern Shore of Virginia (Accomack and Northampton Counties) with the mainland of Virginia to the south and the State of Maryland to the northeast. It provides a direct connection to Route 175, the only access road to Chincoteague Island and the Virginia section of Assateague Island. On the Eastern Shore, Route 13 is a four-lane arterial with a variable-width median separating northbound and southbound traffic throughout most of the corridor.

In 2002, VDOT conducted a study of the Route 13 corridor within the Eastern Shore, including the portion of Route 175 from Route 13 to the entrance of the NASA facility at Wallops Island. The study indicated that annual average daily traffic volumes on Route 13 in both directions ranged from 1,600 to 1,800 vehicles per day, with seasonal variance of the highest volumes in June, July, and August.

To quantify the operating conditions of a highway or intersection, traffic congestion is defined in terms of level of service (LOS) as defined by the Highway Capacity Manual. Level of service is expressed in a range from "A" for excellent conditions to "F" for failing conditions. LOS is determined by measuring the average vehicle delay at intersections, the speed of traffic flow, and mobility between lanes. Despite seasonal variations and high traffic volumes, VDOT's report concluded that "LOS A operating conditions were determined to occur" for U.S. Route 13.[22]

However, the study included several findings and recommendations for improving circulation in its study area, which will be covered in Chapter 3. The study did result in the installation of a traffic signal at the intersection of Routes 175 and 798 (Atlantic Road) near the NASA Wallops Flight Facility after the study determined the intersection was functioning at a poor level of service (LOS E for northbound and LOS F for southbound)

2. Route 175 Causeway and Bridge

Route 175 runs east across the Delmarva Peninsula from Route 13 to the Town of Chincoteague, crossing over the Wire Narrows and Black Narrows Salt Marshes. From Route 13, Route 175 is a two-lane road with no shoulders until its intersection with Route 679, where the road broadens to include paved shoulders until it reaches the shore. The John Whealton Memorial Causeway ("Route 175 Causeway"), built in 1922, is a 2.5-mile stretch of two-lane road with no shoulders and a limited number of pull-off zones (see Figure 9). The Causeway connects to Chincoteague Island via Marsh Island and a drawbridge over the Chincoteague Channel (Figure 10). There is one parking area off of the Causeway, at Queen Sound Landing, for fishing and boat launching. The speed limit is 55 MPH between the mainland and Queen Sound Landing and 45 MPH between the Landing and Chincoteague. There are passing zones along the length of the Causeway. Safety is a concern on the Causeway, most recently highlighted by a fatality at the Queens Sound turnoff in 2007.

VDOT is currently rebuilding the Chincoteague Channel Route 175 Bridge to realign it with Maddox Boulevard, almost one-half mile north of its current terminus between Cleveland and Mumford Streets (just south of Church Street). The realignment may improve the level of service for the bridge and North Main Street, but it may also reduce the level of service for those intersections along Maddox Boulevard, diverting traffic away from using Church Street as a secondary route to CNWR. This project and its effects on traffic are described in more detail in Chapter 3.

Figure 9. Route 175 Causeway (looking west toward the mainland).

Source: Volpe Center, photograph, July 2009.

---

[22] Virginia Department of Transportation. Route 13/Wallops Island Access Management Study. May 2002. http://virginiadot.org/projects/resources/hampton_roads/rte13_final_report.pdf

Figure 10. Route 175 Drawbridge (cars waiting to leave Chincoteague).

Source: Volpe Center, photograph, July 2009.

3. Local roads

The road network in the Town of Chincoteague consists of two-lane commercial and residential streets with varying levels of traffic and service. Circulation on local roadways features local and non-local traffic accessing residential, commercial, and recreational destinations.

According to an earlier Chincoteague *Comprehensive Plan* (2006), most non-local traffic entering the Town of Chincoteague from Route 175 travels north on Main Street, then east on Maddox Boulevard towards Assateague Island. Another major portion of non-local traffic travels down South Main Street to the campgrounds.

VDOT tracks Average Annual Daily Traffic (AADT) to measure the volume of traffic on selected roadways. Map 7 shows available AADT data from 2007 in key Chincoteague locations. Note that neither VDOT nor the Town of Chincoteague has seasonal counts for these roadways.

Data available for Chincoteague from 2007 confirm the travel patterns identified by the Chincoteague *Comprehensive Plan* and also identify a secondary route to CNWR and ASIS, from North Main Street to Church Street to Chicken City Road to Maddox Boulevard. The AADTs on both routes exceed 3000 vehicles per day. The highest AADT within the Town is 9,600 vehicles per day on North Main Street between the Route 175 Bridge and Church Street, which is the first street segment between the Route 175 Bridge and either of the two major routes to CNWR.

Map 7. 2007 Chincoteague AADT.

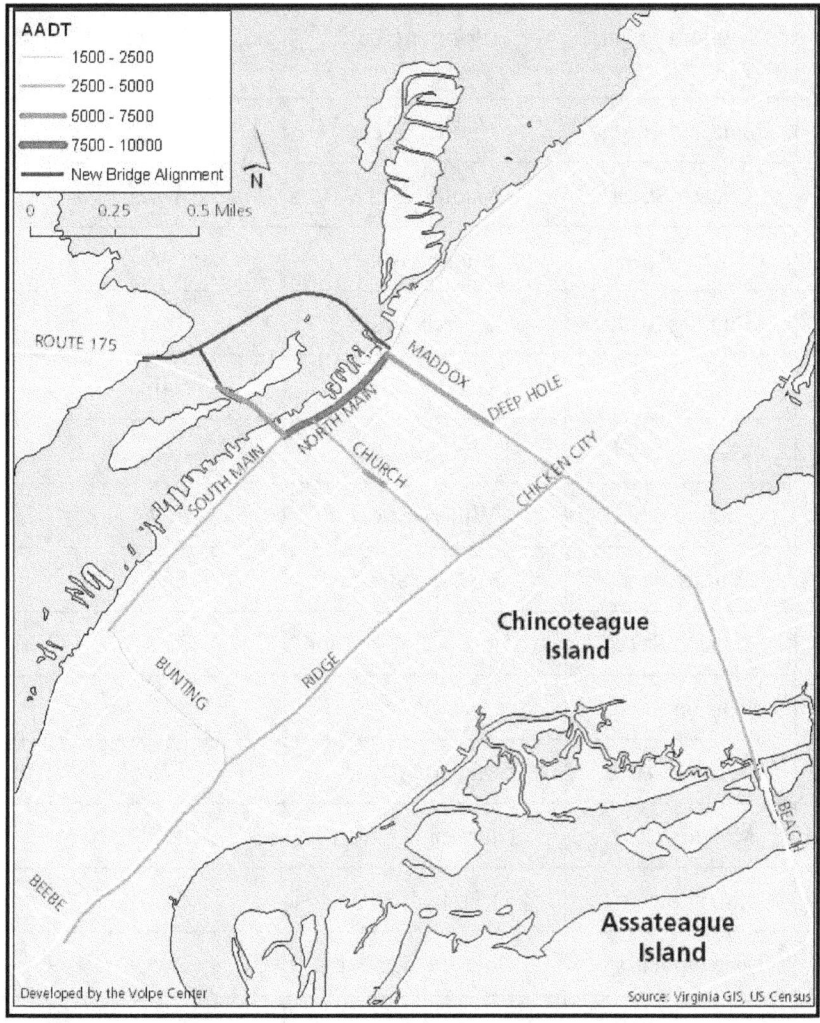

Source: Volpe Center with data from VDOT.

The Virginia Department of Transportation's *2025 State Highway Plan*[23] (the Plan) was consulted as a resource for determining existing operation conditions on roadways in the Town of Chincoteague. The Plan provides a summary of solutions for interstate and primary highway deficiencies on a statewide basis. To prioritize solutions, VDOT provides estimates of operating conditions based upon needs analysis traffic forecasts as part of its Statewide Planning System. According to VDOT, all of Chincoteague's road facilities were operating at good levels of service based on 2007 traffic forecasts. Table 2 summarizes the analysis results, including peak hour traffic flow rates by roadway segment and operating level of service, for routes accessing CNWR.

---

[23] http://virginiadot.org/projects/resources/Virginia2025StateHighwayPlanTechReport.pdf

Table 2. Level of Service.

Road Name	Segment From	Segment To	2007 Flow Rate	Operating Level of Service (2007)
North Main Street	Route 175 Bridge	Church Street	480	C
North Main Street	Church Street	Maddox Blvd.	484	C
Ridge Road	Beebe Road	Bunting Road	176	B
Ridge Road	Bunting Road	Church Street	168	B
Chicken City Rd.	Church Street	Maddox Blvd.	240	A
Chicken City Rd.	Maddox Blvd.	Deep Hole Road	94	A
Church Street	Main Street	Willow Street	167	A
Church Street	Willow Street	Pension Street	267	B
Church Street	Pension Street	0.15 mi east of Pension	222	B
Deep Hole Road	Pension Street	Ocean Avenue	148	A
Deep Hole Road	Ocean Avenue	Maddox Blvd.	146	B
Deep Hole Road	Maddox Blvd.	Chicken City Rd.	137	B
Maddox Blvd.	Main Street	Deep Hole Road	312	B
Maddox Blvd.	Deep Hole Road	Chicken City Rd.	265	B
Maddox Blvd.	Chicken City Rd.	Entrance Assateague Island	372	B

4. CNWR roads

CNWR is accessed by a two-lane road, Beach Road, which extends from Maddox Boulevard across the bridge to the beach parking areas (see Figure 11). Anecdotal evidence suggests that beach traffic backups on peak days can occur from the fee booths to the traffic circle at the entrance to CNWR and ASIS (approximately one quarter mile) and from the beach parking lots to about the Woodland Trail (approximately one mile). CNWR staff indicate that these backups typically occur ten to twenty days per year, on summer weekends, Fourth of July, and Labor Day.

Figure 11. Beach Road Proximate to NPS Visitor Center at Toms Cove.

Source: Volpe Center, photograph, July 2009.

Within CNWR, there is only one additional paved road that is accessible to the public. Wildlife Loop is approximately three miles in length and is open to vehicles after 3 pm each day. There is also a service road that extends north from the Wildlife Loop seven and a half miles, providing access to one of the areas where the Chincoteague ponies are kept. A four to six mile section is open to private vehicles only during part of Waterfowl Week at the end of November but the CNHA bus tour is allowed to use this same section throughout its season of operation. In 2009, due to the damage from the Nor'easter Ida, the service road was not opened to the public during Waterfowl Week.

Transportation Safety

Transportation safety is a paramount concern for CNWR and for the other ATPPL co-applicants. There are no indications that safety of existing transit services has been a concern. However, roadway safety is an issue in the project area and it will grow in importance as road-sharing by alternative and non-motorized transport modes increases.

According to VDOT, there have been between 20 to 50 crashes a year in the Town of Chincoteague over the last five years. A third of these crashes resulted in injuries, with very few due to the use of alcohol. Chincoteague experienced one traffic fatality in 2003, one in the summer of 2007, and two in the winter of 2007-8.[24] The summer 2007 fatality occurred on the Route 175 Causeway. An 11-year-old native of Chincoteague was killed and ten people injured in a three-vehicle accident near Queen Sound Bridge when a car waiting to make a left-hand turn into the parking area was struck from behind. Neither alcohol nor weather was considered factors in the accident.[25] VDOT reports that nineteen total accidents occurred between 2004 and 2007 along the Causeway, three of which were at the site of the August 2007 accident,

---

[24] VA Dept of Motor Vehicles: Virginia Crash Facts, http://www.dmv.state.va.us/webdoc/safety/crash_data/crash_facts/index.asp and CNWR staff.

[25] Furness, Stephen, "Boy, 11, dies in causeway crash", Chincoteague Beacon. August 8, 2007.

with driver error listed as a contributing factor in all cases.[26] Bicycle and pedestrian safety statistics for the Town are not currently available.

A review of CNWR traffic violations records revealed that speeding is the most common infraction, followed by parking violations and vehicle extractions from sand. The number of accidents – between wildlife and vehicles, vehicles, bicycles and vehicles, and pedestrian and vehicles – were minimal. The only trend that emerged from the past five years (2004-2008) was that wildlife-vehicle accidents have been decreasing each year, from 11 in 2004 to 2 in 2008.[27]

Parking

1. Beach parking and management

There are four unpaved parking lots on the eastern side of Assateague Island at the end of Beach Road (Figure 12). The CNWR *Master Plan* (1993) references 961 existing spaces on the beach. Parking at the beach lots is sufficient for most days of the year. Occasionally the lots reach capacity resulting in temporary closures. In addition, storm events can temporarily close the lots due to overwash and subsequent restoration efforts. The storm event of November 2009 washed out and buried the parking lots, resulting in a possible long-term closure.

Figure 12. CNWR Beach Parking Lot.

Source: Volpe Center, photograph, July 2009.

From 1982 to 2001, CNWR and ASIS kept records of when the beach parking lots reached capacity (see Figure 13). A review of data from 2000 and 2001 indicates that closures last from thirty minutes to four hours and were always initiated between 11:00 am and 2:00 pm. There are no similar records for 2001 to 2008, but CNWR staff anecdotally reported that there are typically four to six closures a year, also occurring between the peak hours noted above, and lasting approximately thirty minutes to two hours. These closures are highly weather-dependent but usually occur on the 4th of July if it is a three-day weekend, and on the first two Saturdays and Sundays in August. In 2009, the Refuge reported thirteen closures due to the parking reaching capacity, with an additional two closures due to storm events.

---

[26] Vaughn, Carol, "Accomack Board Denies Bike Lane Study Despite Boy's Death", December 21, 2007. http://www.vabike.org/accomac-denies-bike-lane-study/

[27] Law Enforcement Data provided by CNWR, October 2008.

Figure 13. CNWR Entrance Closures Due to Full Beach Parking Lots.

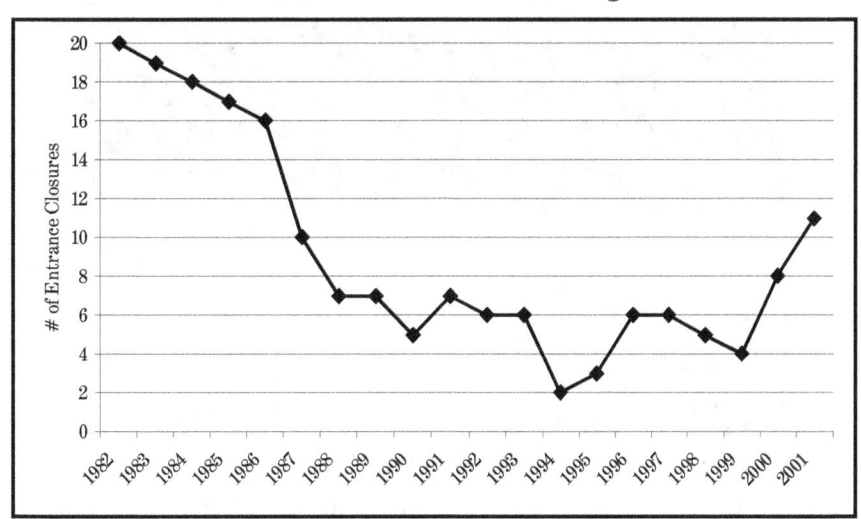

Source: Volpe Center with data from ASIS staff.

Maintenance of the unpaved beach parking lots is a major ASIS activity supported by NPS operations funds as well as in part by CNWR entrance fees. The lots require routine maintenance twice weekly April through November and weekly December through March, consisting of removing wind-blown or over-washed beach sand (Figures 14 and 15), filling washouts or smoothing washboard parking lots and roads, and adding and leveling crushed-shell. The estimated annual cost for this work is $7,200 in labor (assuming 4 hours per day at $20/hour), but there are also additional costs for the fuel and for the purchase and maintenance of a 3/4 ton pick-up with drag attachment.

The beach parking lots also sustain average annual storm damage of $150,000, with a range of $100,000 to $600,000. Repairing the damage from the November 2009 storm event was roughly estimated to cost $600,000 to $900,000. The length of time needed for storm repairs varies from two weeks to three months. These repairs have ranged from fixing washed-out parking lots and roads to total relocation of parking lots and roads slightly to the west. CNWR and ASIS staff believe that such damage could be significantly reduced if the parking lots were relocated to areas less prone to the impacts of coastal storms and future sea level rise.

Figure 14. Overwash of Beach Parking Areas.

Source: CNWR staff (date unknown).

Figure 15. Damage and Clean-up of Parking Areas 2-4.

Source: Patrick J. Hendrickson, Highcamera.com (9-30-08). Provided by CNWR staff.

As mentioned in Chapter 1, a new fee proposal was implemented in 2008 in part so that a portion of the additional revenues could be transferred to the National Park Service (NPS) each year to help offset maintenance cost of beach parking facilities and safety services. The proposed fee changes were introduced to the public in 2007 with meetings and an invitation to submit comments. The majority of public comments received indicated that the proposed fee increase in the Virginia area of the ASIS should be charged as part of the existing CNWR entrance fees and not a separate NPS daily parking fee. Additionally, the comments strongly supported the position that any new fees should be earmarked to help defray the maintenance cost for beach parking and other visitor safety services. After consideration of public concerns, both agencies agreed that it would benefit the visitor to increase CNWR's current fees to help the NPS recover the costs of providing beach parking and visitor safety services.

In 2008, total revenues were approximately $700,000, a decrease of almost $20,000 (5 percent) from 2007, despite the new fee structure and a two percent increase in visits. It is possible that visitors who previously purchased weekly ($10), annual ($30), or senior ($10) passes purchased the daily pass ($5) as a less expensive option, thus resulting in lower total revenue. Nearly 40 percent of CNWR's annual revenue from entrance fees came from daily passes in 2008. Figure 16 shows the change in the types of passes sold between 2007 and 2008. Figure 17 shows revenues by fee type for the same years.

During 2008, CNWR received nearly $85,000 from the "new" parking fees (the $15 amenity fee for the CNWR annual pass and Federal Duck Stamp; 64 percent of Duck Stamp purchasers bought the parking pass). Since these fees were not introduced at the beginning of the year, this number does not reflect the full potential for annual revenue. In comparison, also during 2008, CNWR transferred $230,000 to the NPS for the maintenance of the beach parking lots and for visitor safety services, including life guarding and law enforcement. Thus, the designated parking fees covered less than half of the costs.

Due to the miscalculation of the impact of the new fee structure on revenues, CNWR is increasing the daily fee pass from $5 to $8 in 2010; this will provide an incentive for anyone visiting more than one day to purchase the weekly pass (as two daily passes would cost $16, more than the $15 weekly pass).

More detailed ASIS/CNWR parking information and data appear in Appendix B.

Figure 16. Number of Passes Sold by Type, 2007-08.

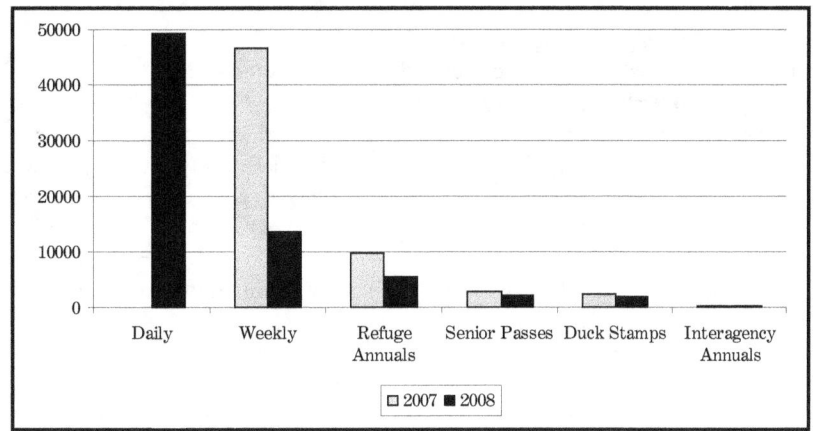

Source: CNWR data.

Figure 17. Revenues by Fee Type, 2007-08.

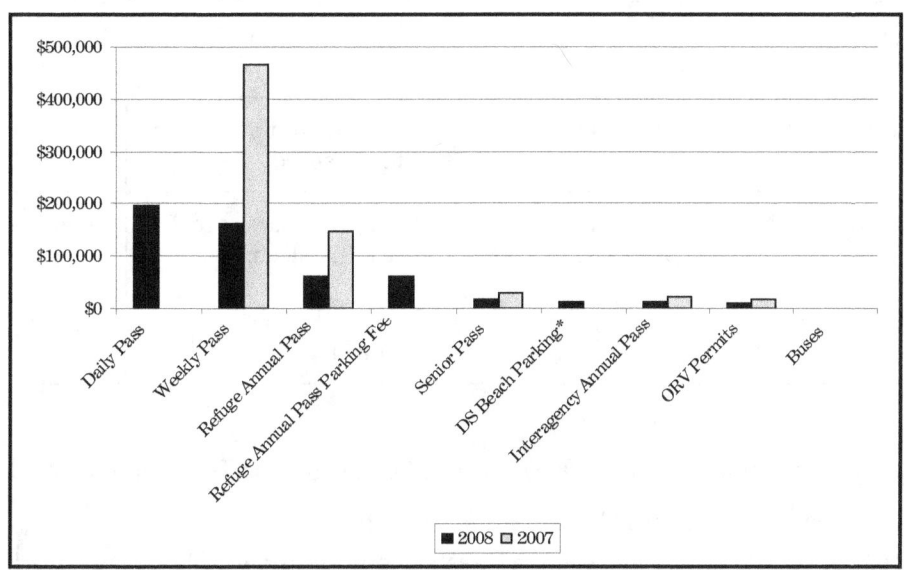

Source: CNWR data.

2. Other parking on Assateague Island (Virginia)

Information on parking elsewhere in the Virginia District of Assateague Island including CNWR appears in Table 3.

Table 3. Non-beach Parking Facilities on Assateague Island (Virginia section).

Lot Location	Paved, Marked Spaces	Handicapped Spaces (paved and marked)	Other spaces	Bus/Oversize Parking Spaces
Bateman Center	52	4	23 regular; 6 for Govt. (unpaved, car stops)	Gravel area for oversized vehicles and bus parking
Wildlife Loop (Main lot)	38	1	5 (paved but unmarked)	3 paved
Woodland Trail	26	1	None	None
Lighthouse Trail	17	None	6 (paved, unmarked)	2 (paved, unmarked)
Wildlife Loop (Near boardwalk)	7	1	None	None
Boat ramp, west side	None	None	12 (paved, unmarked)	None
Light Keepers House	None	None	15 spaces (unpaved) –for handicapped	None
NPS Toms Cove Visitor Center	None	2 (unpaved but marked)	~50, both sides of road (unmarked, unpaved)	None
TOTAL	140	9	~1,050	~5

3. Town parking

The Chincoteague *Comprehensive Plan* (2009) cataloged parking in the Town, and reported that:

- Parking in the downtown area (Main Street) is limited
- The area between Mumford and Church Streets allows some curbside/on-street parking on the east side of Main Street
- The Town owns and maintains a parking lot off of Post Office Street between Mumford and Church Streets
- The Town also provides off-street parking in the boat ramp area located across from the Chincoteague Volunteer Fire Company's main station.

In addition, the Town Planner reported that on-street parking in Chincoteague is free and is available on most roadways in Town although there are locations where on-street parking should be restricted for safety reasons due to limited shoulder width.

Table 4 and Map 8 identify the Town of Chincoteague's main public parking locations and capacities.

Table 4. Public Parking in the Town of Chincoteague.

Parking Area	Number of Spaces
Chincoteague High School	157
Chincoteague Elementary School	77
Chincoteague Community Center	221 (including 8 handicapped)
Post Office Street Parking Lot	59
Carnival Overflow Parking	Approximately 100

Map 8. Chincoteague Public Parking.

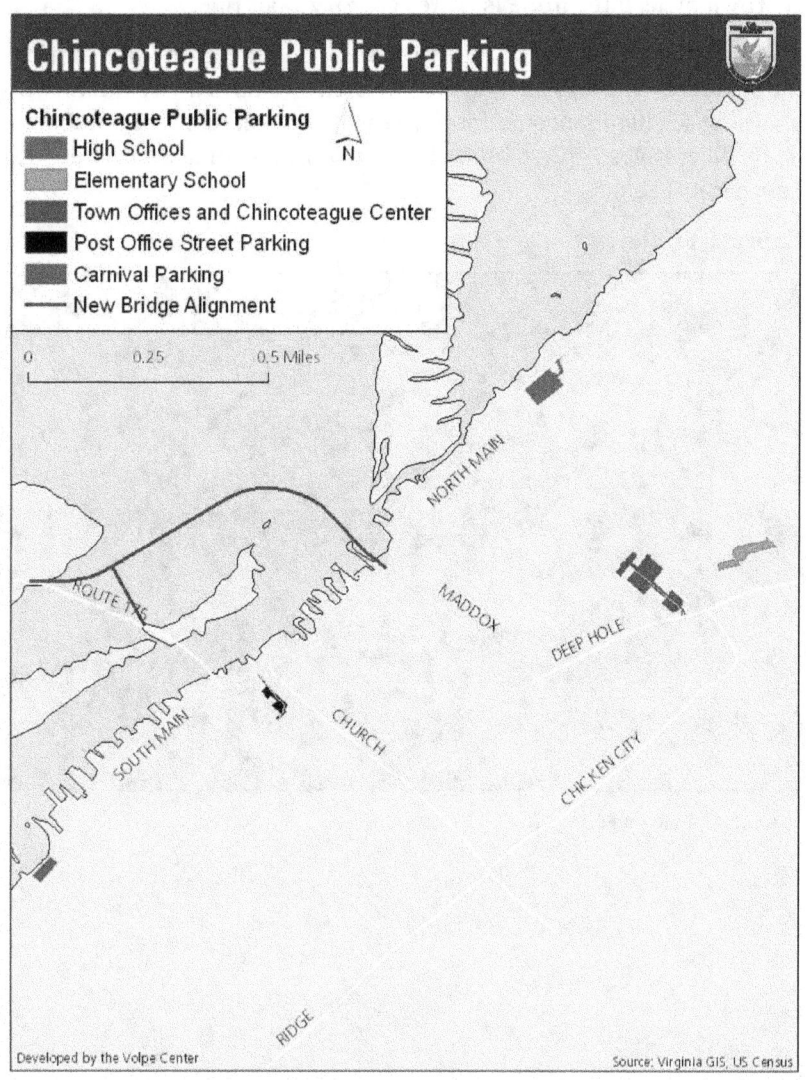

Source: Volpe Center, using State of Virginia and ASIS data.

4. NASA Visitor Center parking

NASA's Wallops Flight Facility Visitor Center, located 11 miles west of CNWR along Route 175, has a paved lot that can accommodate 44 regular vehicles and two full-size buses and an overflow lot in a nearby field that can accommodate approximately 40 regular vehicles. The visitor facility has never closed due to lack of parking.

Transit

1. Pony Express Trolley Service

The Pony Express is a seasonal trolley service operated by the Town of Chincoteague that serves primary community and tourist sites throughout the Town (see Figure 18). Trolley management reported that in 2005, popular destinations or "hot spots" were the island's ice cream parlors and downtown on Main Street.[28] The service runs in the evening (approximately 5:00 pm to 10:30 pm) every day from Memorial Day through the end of August, with extended evening hour service offered during peak times. The service also operates on the weekends in September and October (see schedule in Figure 19 and service map in Map 9). The Town owns three trolleys. Fares are $0.25 per ride.

The Pony Express trolleys are also used by the History Tour Volunteers for an historical tour Wednesday afternoons during the summer. In 2007, the tour was offered two days a week, rather than one, and attracted 866 riders, raising $2,404 in income for the Town.[29] Adult fares are $3.00 and reduced fares ($2.00) are available for riders ages 2-12. Children under two years of age ride free. Ridership data for 2004 through 2009 appear in Table 5.

Figure 18. Pony Express Trolley.

Source: Volpe Center, photograph, July 2009.

---

[28] Furness, Stephen. Chincoteague Beacon. November 3, 2005.

[29] December 3, 2007 Town Council Meeting. http://www.chincoteaguereports.com/my_weblog/chincoteague-town-council/page/2/

Figure 19. Pony Express Schedule.

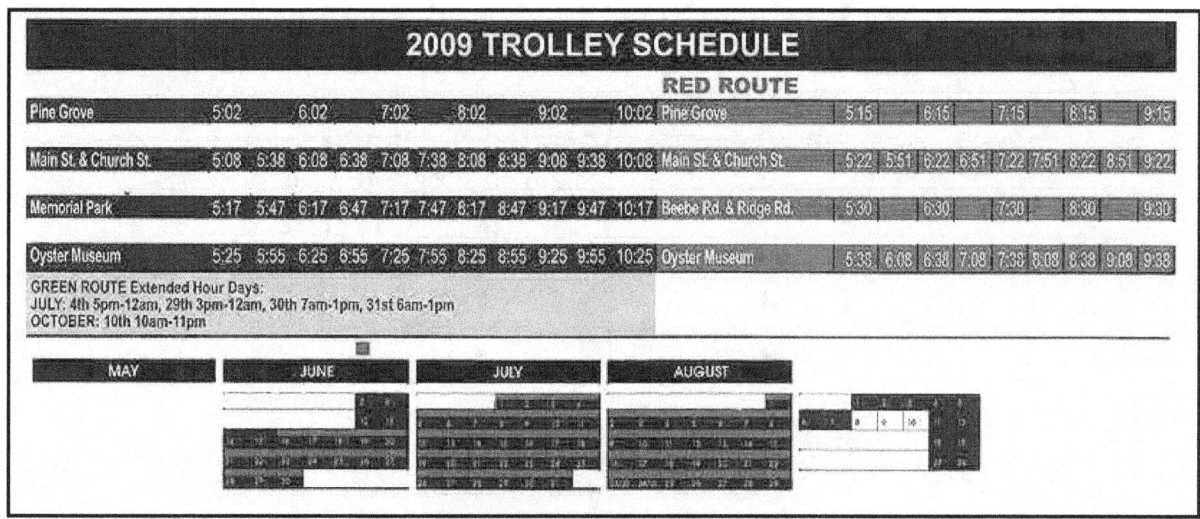

Source: Town of Chincoteague.

Map 9: Map of Pony Express Trolley Service.

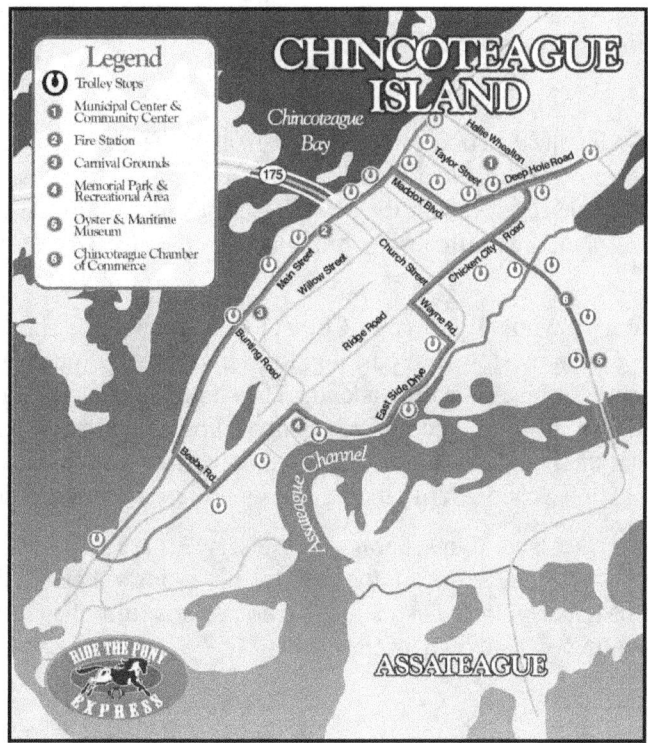

Source: Town of Chincoteague.

Table 5. Trolley Ridership Information 2004-2009.

Year	Passenger Trips
2004	9,682
2005	7,691
2006	12,502
2007	15,302
2008	13,934
2009 (estimated)	14,500

Source: Town of Chincoteague Newsletter. January 14, 2009. http://www.chincoteague-va.gov/announcements/January%20Newsletter%2009.pdf.

The *Chincoteague Beacon* noted in February 2008 that residents do not think there are enough riders to support the service, especially in relation to its cost.[30] However, there was response to the project outreach effort for this study that the trolleys are well used, predominantly by visitors but also by residents, especially children and mobility-challenged people.

2. Shuttle Services during Annual Pony Swim & Auction

During the Annual Pony Swim and Auction each July, the Town offers a special shuttle services on specific days to help reduce congestion and address parking scarcity at key sites. In 2009, for the first time, CNHA offered a $5 shuttle service from the FWS Visitor Center to the Swans Cove Trailhead on the day of the Beach Walk, when the north herd is brought from the north down the beach to the pony corrals off of Beach Road.

On the day of the annual Pony Swim, the Town of Chincoteague runs a free shuttle service from Chincoteague High School, the only stop with parking, to Memorial Park, near the site of the Pony Swim, where the ponies come ashore from Assateague Island. The shuttle makes several other stops within Town (Map 10). The shuttle consists of Accomack County school buses and a rented handicapped-accessible vehicle (note that the Pony Express trolleys maintain their scheduled service). Buses begin operation at 5 am from the High School. Volunteer guides are present on each bus.

Once the ponies have all reached land, two separate shuttle services are provided: one express bus from Memorial Park to the Carnival Grounds and another bus from Memorial Park to the High School. The buses continue to run until Memorial Park has cleared. The last bus from the Carnival Grounds departs at approximately 2 pm, depending on actual swim time.

---

[30] Furness, Stephen. Chincoteague Beacon. February 5, 2008.

Map 10. Pony Swim Shuttle Route.

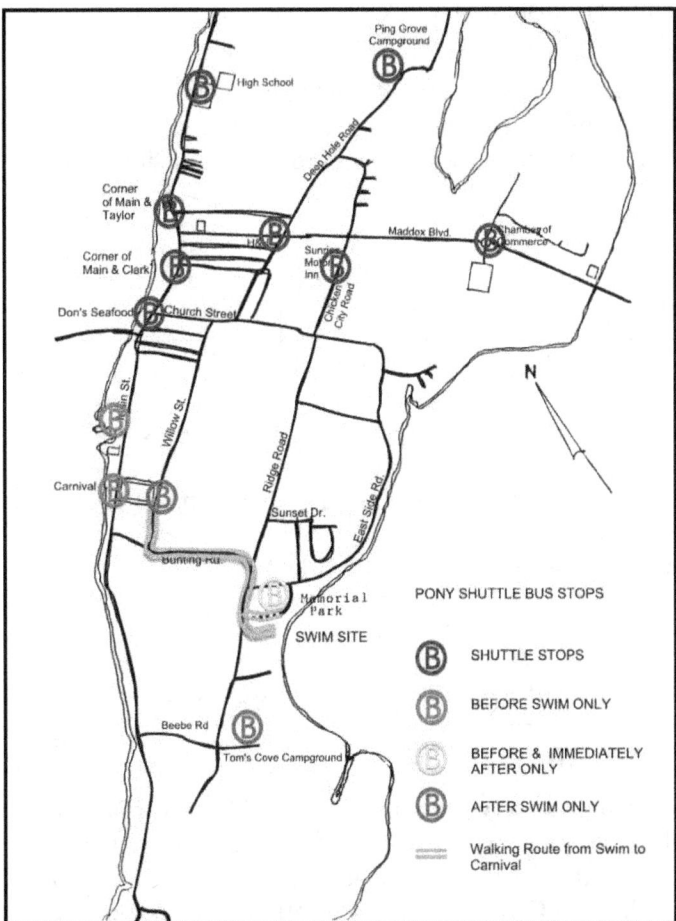

Source: Town of Chincoteague website. http://www.chincoteague-va.gov/visitors/pony%20swim%20shuttle%20stop%20map.shtm.

3. CNHA Bus Tour

The Chincoteague Natural History Association (CNHA) provides a seasonal, interpretive bus tour service within CNWR under a cooperative agreement. The service began in 2004 after completion of a compatibility determination, which included public outreach and a public comment period and determined that it helped achieve one of CNWR's purposes, to provide opportunities for the public to develop an understanding and appreciation for wildlife. As a nonprofit enterprise, CNHA uses proceeds collected from the tour to support its interpretation services. According to CNWR records, similar tours had been operated within CNWR by various outfitters between 1970 and 2001, but were suspended until CNHA took over operations.

The tour operates from April through November and takes visitors to a part of the island that is not publically accessible by vehicles, including one of the best locations to see the Chincoteague ponies. The tour departs from the CNWR Lighthouse landing and boat launch parking area (on the west side) and travels to the end of the service road and back, a distance of approximately fifteen miles round trip. The tour lasts 1.5 hours and is accompanied by an interpreter/guide who provides information about wildlife and ecology. The cost in 2009 was $12 for adults, $8 for CNHA members (except July and August), and $6 for children ages 2 to 12. Group rates and special tours are available by request. Table 6 shows the 2008 tour schedule.

The CNHA operates a used, 32-seat bus equipped with air conditioning and a wheelchair lift. CNHA contracts with a small company, Eastern Shore Action, to provide drivers and ensure that the service complies with VDOT safety requirements.

According to its business manager, CNHA provides tours for 6,000 to 10,000 people each year. Most riders are repeat customers interested in viewing the Chincoteague ponies. In 2008, there was a decrease in customers attributed largely to the economic downturn. CNHA is interested in increasing its ridership for the tour.

Table 6. CNHA Tour Schedule (2009).

Month	Tours
April	Saturday 1:00 PM, Sunday 10:00 AM
May	Friday 4:00 PM, Saturday 1:00 PM, Sunday 10:00 AM
June	Thursday thru Monday 10:00 AM and 4:00 PM
July & August	Daily 10:00 AM and 4:00 PM
September	Thursday thru Monday 10:00 AM
October/November	Saturday 1:00 PM, Sunday 10:00 AM

4. STAR Transit

STAR Transit provides regional bus service within Accomack and Northampton counties with racks for bicycles on all buses. The Blue Route has provided service from Onley to Chincoteague since 1996 with service to three destinations in the Town: Chincoteague Center, the intersection of Maddox Boulevard and Deep Hole Road, and the Post Office Street Town parking lot (see service map, Map 11). Service is infrequent, with three daily runs between 6:00 AM and 3:00 PM, and the total duration for the ride from the Chincoteague Center to Onley is approximately 1.5 hours. Average monthly ridership for the route is 500 to 600. Fares are $1.50 and children less than four are free; reduced fares are available for individuals 62 years and over and qualified ADA disabled passengers.

5. Hotel-run transit service proposal

In 2005, the Mariner Motel proposed a shuttle service for motel patrons to and from the Assateague beach in an airport-type bus, with hourly pick-ups and drop-offs, from Memorial Day to Labor Day. The CNWR planned to require a special-use permit for its operation with a $250 fee.

CNWR and ASIS planned to expand the turn circle at the beach to make a pull-off lane to accommodate three hotel shuttles at a time. Shuttle runs would be reduced when the beach parking lots were full so as not to overcrowd the beach. At a May 2005 public meeting held to discuss the proposal, some attendees reported that similar ideas had been considered by other motels in the previous year. At the meeting, concern was expressed about setting a precedent for more motel shuttle services, endangering the fragile nature of CNWR, and the problems associated with storm evacuation. As a result of these concerns, the Motel did not pursue the service further.[31]

---

[31] Furness, Stephen. Refuge will experiment with hotel taxi services. Chincoteague Beacon. May 12, 2005.

Map 11. Map of STAR Transit Blue Route.

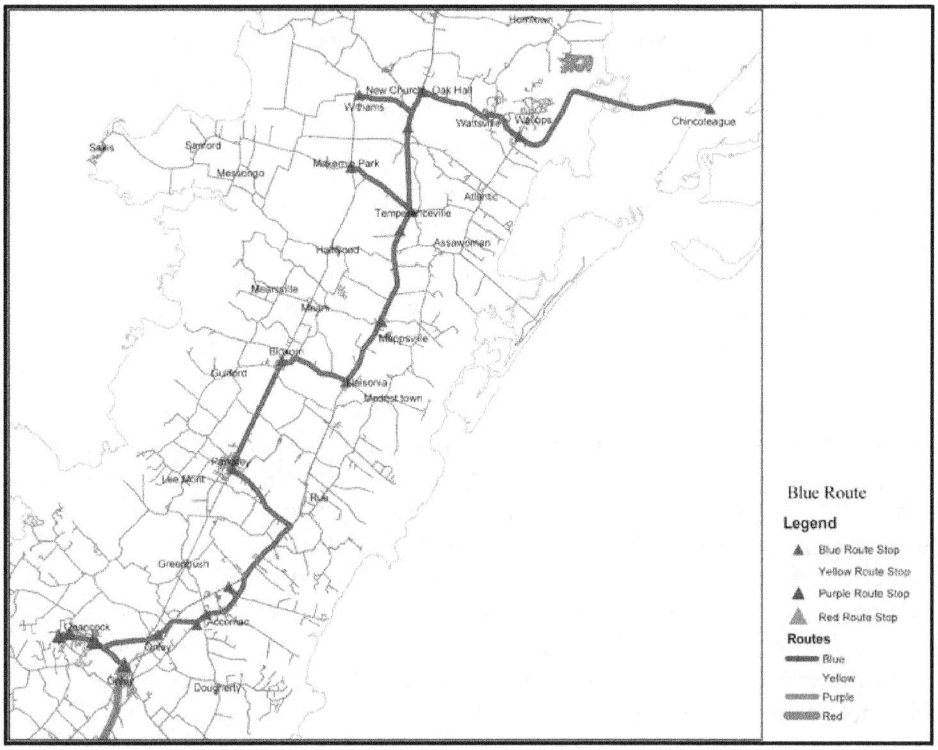

Source: STAR Transit website, http://www.mystartransit.com.

6. Other transit proposals

Two previous transportation plans proposed transit systems to provide access between locations in the Town and CNWR. The *Assateague Island Transportation Study* prepared by Vollmer Associates (1976) advocated employing retired British double-decker buses to run three different 30-minute routes from the beach to points of lodging (motels and campgrounds) in Chincoteague and a parking facility on Maddox Boulevard between the traffic circle and CNWR. The *Analysis of Traffic Management Options Report* prepared by Barry Lawson Associates (1986) similarly outlined various options for shuttles to the beach from off-site parking lots, such as the campground, the CNWR Visitor Center, the Town dump, vacant/available land on Maddox Boulevard or Chicken City Road, and the site of the proposed Community Center, which has since been constructed. These proposals were not implemented.

Bicycle and Pedestrian Activity

Cycling in the Town of Chincoteague and within CNWR is a popular recreational activity for visitors and residents, as well as a mode of transportation for adults and children. According to the Town of Chincoteague's revised bicycle plan[32], CNWR reported 66,924 bicyclists entering CNWR for the 2008 calendar year; a Federal Highway Administration report on bicycling in public lands concluded that Chincoteague NWR had the highest number of bicycle visits (77,044) among all the National Wildlife Refuges in 2004.[33] According to CNWR's FY08 application for FTA funding, the CNWR bicycle trail is used by approximately 700 cyclists per day during peak season.

---

[32] Bicycle Plan. From Meeting Notes of the Recreation & Community Enhancement Committee Meeting, May 19, 2009.

[33] Federal Highway Administration, Central Federal Lands Highway Division. Guide to Promoting Bicycling on Federal Lands. September 2008. www.westerntransportationinstitute.org

The bicycle connection between CNWR and the Town is very important because many bicyclists travel from the Town, where they are staying or where they rent bicycles, into CNWR. Some bicyclists drive into CNWR with their bicycles to park at the Wildlife Loop or one of the other parking areas. Currently there is no designated bicycle path or lane that leads from the Town to CNWR; the existing CNWR bicycle trail only starts at the border between the Town and entrance to CNWR.

1. Bicycling in CNWR

Bicycle use is approved under the CNWR *Master Plan* and is identified as enabling visitors to observe wildlife. A compatibility determination, including public outreach, was conducted in 2004 and received no comments in opposition of the use. Construction of bicycle trails began in the 1970s and 1980s. Currently, CNWR has a paved and gravel bicycle trail that runs from the shore of Chincoteague, across the bridges between Assateague and Chincoteague (Figure 20) to the Woodland Trail parking lot. It begins at the mainland side of the bridge between Chincoteague and Assateague as a paved trail that runs to the Wildlife Loop parking area and shortly beyond, where it then joins the road as a gravel path. The Wildlife Loop itself offers a 3-mile paved loop for exclusive use by bicyclists, runners, and walkers each day before 3:00 pm, after which vehicular traffic is permitted. From the Wildlife Loop, bicyclists can access Beach Road via the paved Black Duck Trail or access the beach via the paved Swan Cove Trail (see trail map, Map 12). The Swan Cove Trail formerly ran south along the beach to the parking lots but CNWR stopped maintaining it after it was repeatedly washed away by wave and sand action. The 2009 nor'easter destroyed any remnants of the trail. In response to the lost connection to the beach parking areas, CNWR provided bicycle parking and an emergency cellular phone booth where the Swan Cove Trail met the beach (see Figure 21); however, the phone service was badly damaged by the 2009 nor'easter and is not operational at this time.

Figure 20. Bicycle Trail Connection from the Town to CNWR.

Source: Volpe Center, photograph, July 2009.

Figure 21. Bicycle Parking and Emergency Facilities at End of Swan Cove Trail.

Source: CNWR, photograph, date unknown.

Map 12. CNWR Trail Map.

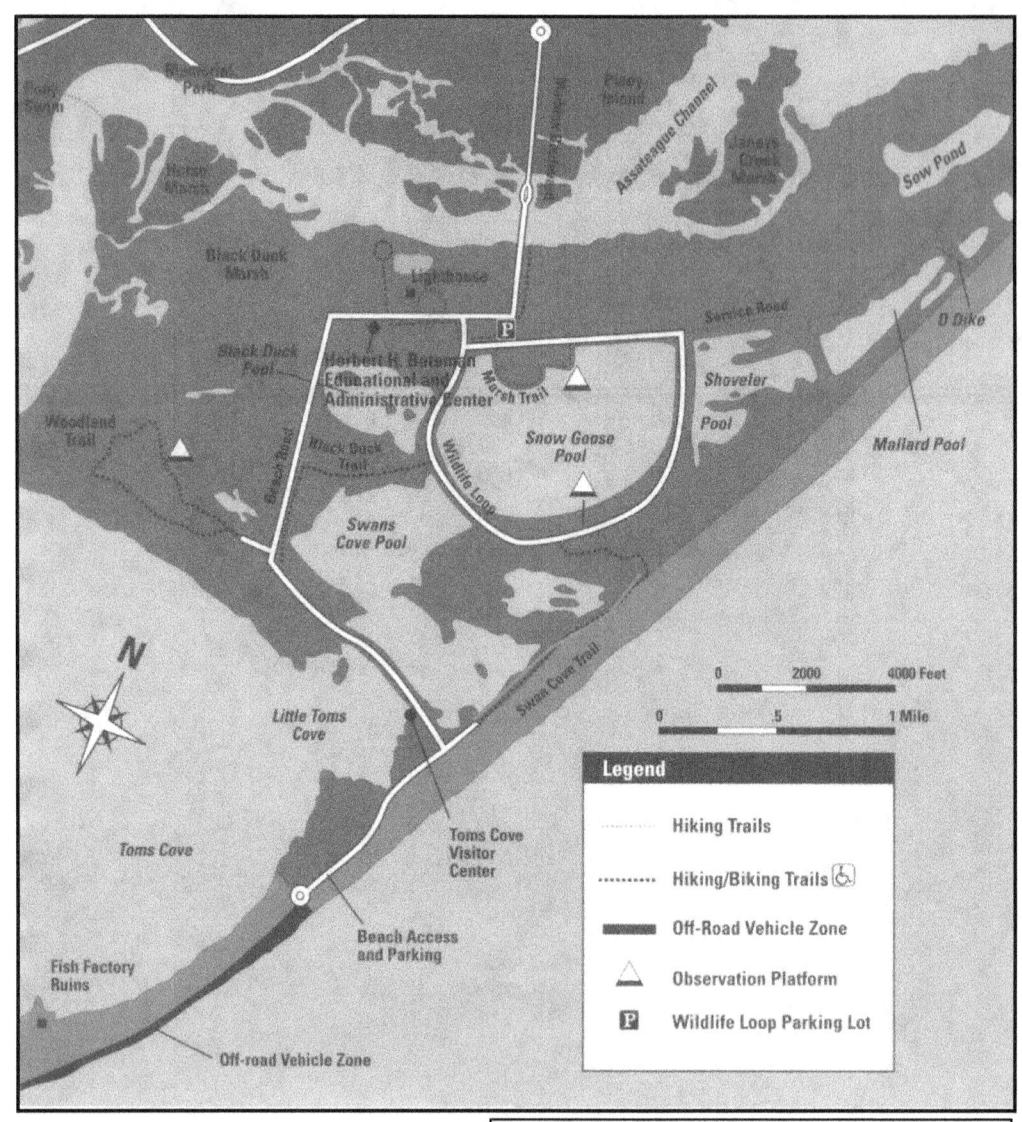

Source: CNWR.

| | Portion of Swan Cove Trail that no longer exists; destroyed by storm overwash |

2. *Bicycling in the Town of Chincoteague*

The Town of Chincoteague currently has limited bicycle infrastructure, including less than one mile of wide shoulders located along Maddox Boulevard between CNWR and Chicken City Road. Elsewhere, there are narrow shoulders or no shoulders at all and bicycles use the travel lanes or the sidewalk (Figure 22). The Town has a bicycle plan, discussed in Chapter 3, and a bicycle map that identifies recommended routes (Map 13). Public bicycle racks are also available in the Town of Chincoteague (Map 14).

Figure 22. Bicycling on Maddox Boulevard Sidewalk in Chincoteague.

Source: Volpe Center, photograph, July 2009.

Map 13. Town of Chincoteague Bicycling Map.

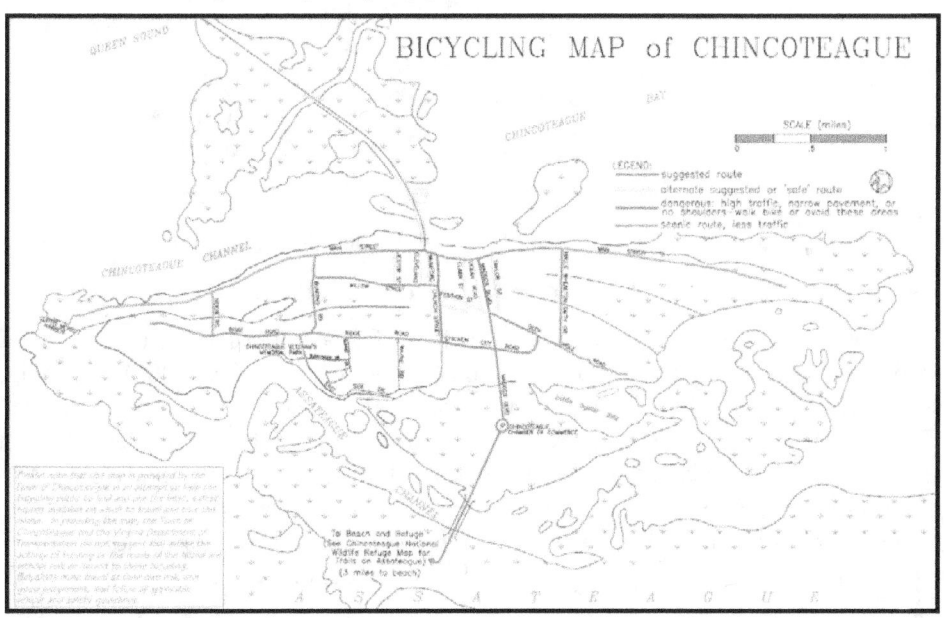

Source: Town of Chincoteague.

Map 14. Chincoteague Bicycle Parking.

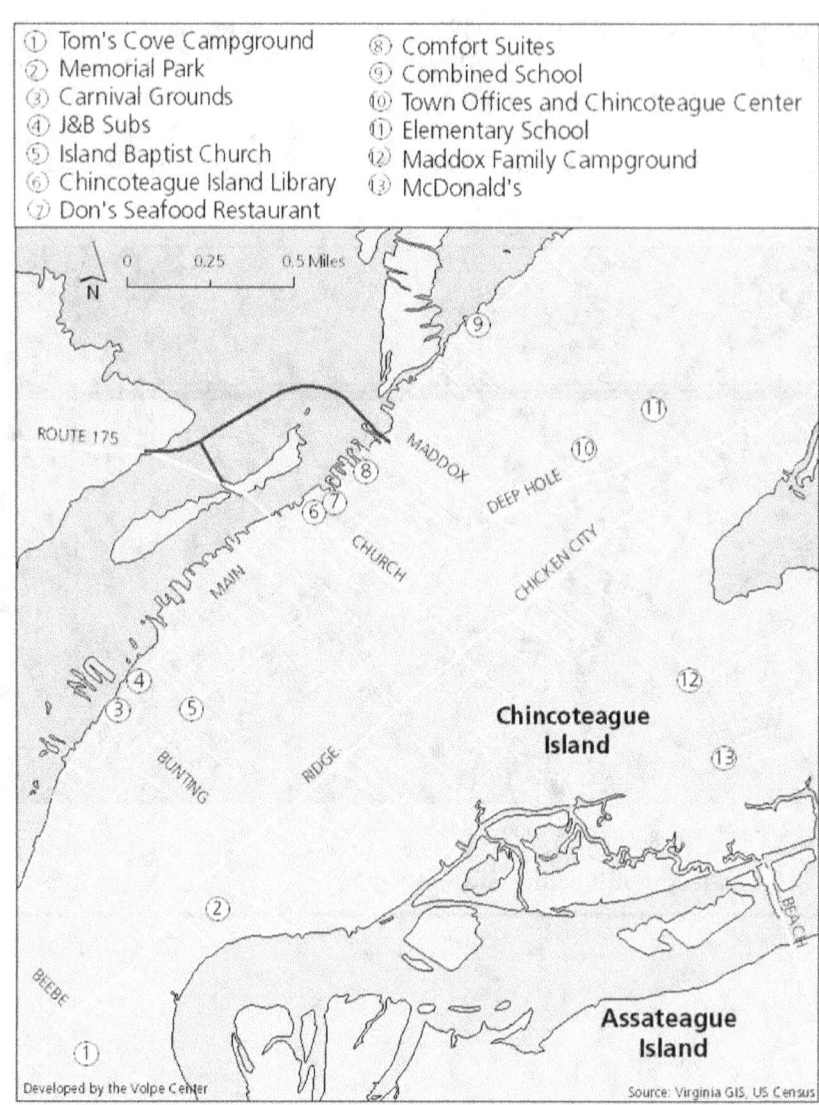

① Tom's Cove Campground
② Memorial Park
③ Carnival Grounds
④ J&B Subs
⑤ Island Baptist Church
⑥ Chincoteague Island Library
⑦ Don's Seafood Restaurant
⑧ Comfort Suites
⑨ Combined School
⑩ Town Offices and Chincoteague Center
⑪ Elementary School
⑫ Maddox Family Campground
⑬ McDonald's

Source: Developed by the Volpe Center with data from the Town of Chincoteague.

3. Town pedestrian activity and facilities

The 2000 U.S. Census indicates that in Chincoteague, about 6.6 percent of workers over the age of 16 travel to work on foot. According to the Chincoteague *Comprehensive Plan* (2009), approximately 80 percent of the public roads serving residential and commercial areas in the downtown area have sidewalks. The *Chincoteague 2020 Transportation Plan* provides details of the sidewalk locations including the western end of Maddox Boulevard and several other side streets connecting to Main Street. There are limited sidewalks in the annexed area of the Town. In the past, the Town has had a policy of installing sidewalks upon citizen request. The Town annually allocates approximately $2,000 in public funds for the maintenance and extension of these facilities to meet citizen requests or municipal needs.

In 2005, the Town built a nature trail as well as a paved shared use trail, off of Hallie Whealton Smith Drive (Figure 23) near the Elementary School, with the idea of building on the system of trails on Assateague Island.

Alternative Vehicles

The expansion of rental options for small non-motorized and motorized vehicles for visitors and an increase in electric vehicle use, primarily modified golf carts, by residents has resulted in heightened concern about road sharing and road safety in the Town of Chincoteague and on Assateague Island.

Besides a variety of two-wheel bicycles (e.g., recumbent, tandem, side-by-side tandem), visitors to Chincoteague have the opportunity to rent other non-motorized and small motorized vehicles including: mopeds, scooters (Figure 24), four-wheel bicycle surreys, and the Scoot Coupe,[34] a three-wheeled, two-passenger scooter (Figure 25). The Scoot Coupe meets all Federal safety standards for motorcycles and are "street legal" in all 50 states. Depending on the model, the Scoot Coup is classified as either a moped/scooter or motorcycle and operates at a top speed of 30 or 55 MPH, respectively.

Figure 23. Shared use path on Hallie Whealton Smith Drive.

Source: Volpe Center, photograph, July 2009.

Figure 24. Scooters on Main Street, Chincoteague.

Source: Volpe Center, photograph, July 2009.

---

[34] Panther Motors, Inc. website. http://www.scootcoupe.com

Figure 25. Scoot Coupe Entering CNWR on Beach Road and at Rental Place.

Source: Volpe Center, photograph, July 2009.

Marine transportation

The project team investigated the opportunity for including marine transportation elements in the transportation alternatives for CNWR and the Town of Chincoteague. The focus of this effort was to assess the potential of passenger boats to provide transport from the Town to CNWR, in particular the public beach on the ocean front, as an alternative to private vehicle travel to CNWR. The examination included the possibilities of marine service to other points in CNWR, that is, the lighthouse and the old Coast Guard facility on Toms Cove; these would likely be "event" destinations, for example, groups visiting for educational, cultural, and research purposes.

Presentation of the marine transportation mode here departs from those in previous sections in that both the existing situation and prospective for future landing facilities are described. The analysis of the possibility of future services appears in Chapter 6.

1. Overview

The marine sector in the study area includes commercial fishing, fishing charters, excursion services, and both motorized, sailing and paddle recreational boats, typical of many places on the Chesapeake Bay and Delmarva Peninsula. There are, however, no passenger ferry services operating in or around the Town of Chincoteague at this time. Six possible gateway and destination landing sites are identified and described.

The navigation chart that appears in Map 15 shows that Assateague Island, in particular the portion occupied by CNWR, is separated from Chincoteague Island and the Town of Chincoteague by the Assateague Channel, which affords reasonable routes to the west shore of CNWR and Toms Cove. The public marine facilities in Chincoteague are the following, which are identified numerically in Map 15:

1. Curtis Merritt Harbor
2. Chincoteague Municipal docks
3. Chincoteague East Side Drive Landing

The landings of possible interest on Assateague Island, also identified numerically in Map 15, are the following:

4. Existing facility at Assateague Lighthouse landing
5. NPS Visitor Center, Toms Cove (no existing landing facility)
6. Former U.S. Coast Guard Station, Toms Cove Hook (existing facility, in disuse and disrepair)

Map 15. Local Waters and Public Marine Facilities Proximate to CNWR and Town of Chincoteague.

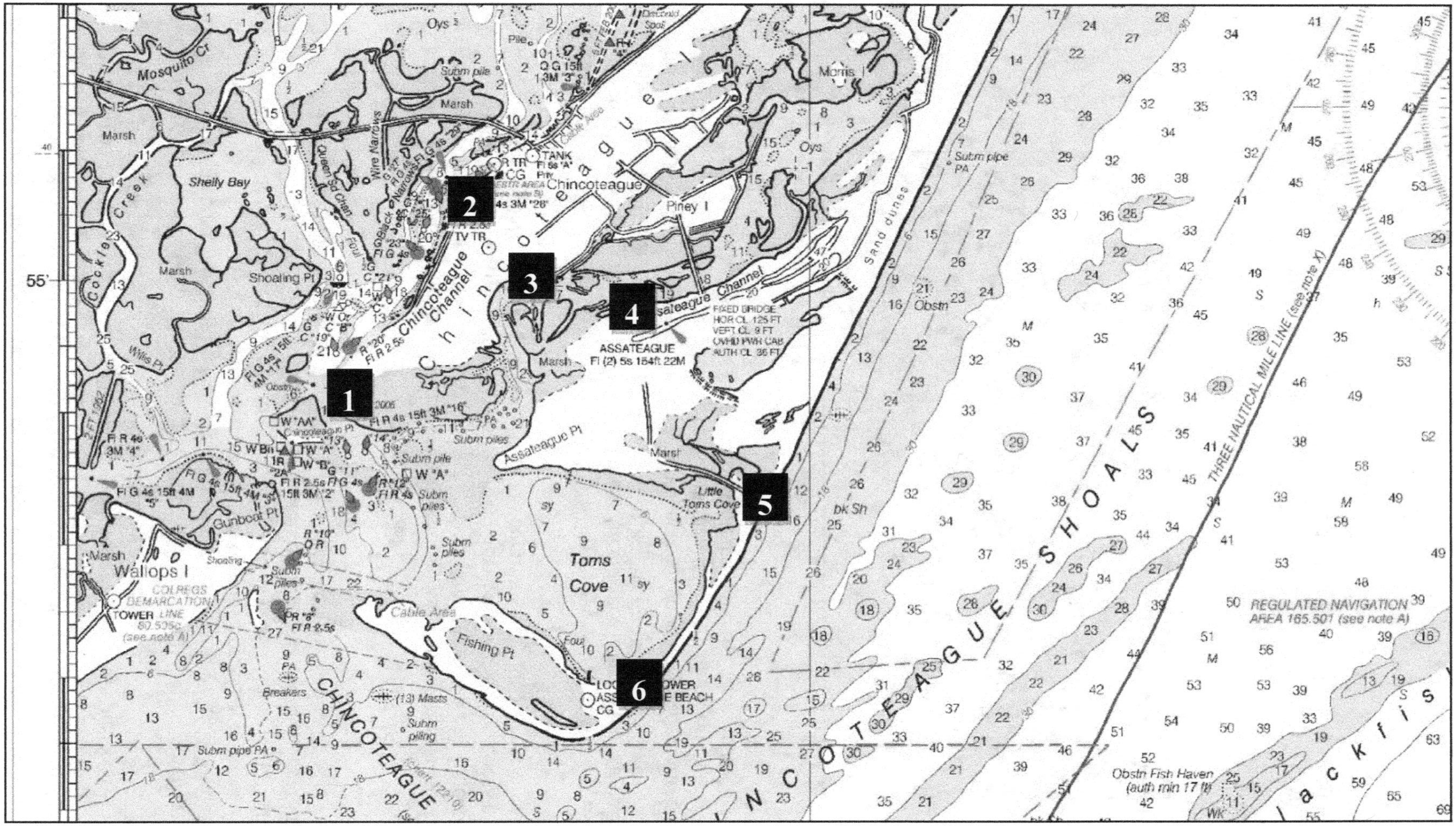

Source: NOAA Chart #1211

49

Currently, operators in Chincoteague offer tours and charter boat rides that operate and depart from Curtis Merritt Harbor and the Chincoteague municipal docks.[35] Popular attractions for the tours include birding, watching the sunset, viewing wildlife and ponies, and fishing. Most tours last one to two hours and cost between $25 and $40 per person. Most of the companies that operate within ASIS have been brought into compliance in recent years with NPS commercial permitting requirements.

Visitors with kayaks or canoes may use the 70-mile long Seaside Water Trail,[36] which was developed by the Accomack-Northampton Planning District Commission in cooperation with Accomack County, Northampton County, the Town of Chincoteague, the Town of Wachapreague, and the Virginia Coastal Zone Management Program. According to the Chincoteague *Comprehensive Plan* (2009), two floating docks have been installed in the Towns of Chincoteague and Wachapreague to provide improved canoe, kayak and public access to the Seaside Water Trail. The Chincoteague floating dock is located at the Town's Eastside Landing Dock off Eastside Landing Road.

1. Town public marine facilities

Curtis Merritt Harbor is a municipally-owned facility providing dockage and service for commercial fishing boats and a marina for recreational boats, located at the southwest end of Chincoteague Island on Route 175 (Main Street). The Town leases 25- to 50-foot slips (Figure 26). The docks and slips have the physical capacity for a small passenger vessel. There are approximately 80-100 parking spaces at Curtis Merritt Harbor, the most of any of the Town departure sites.

Curtis Merritt is the closest facility to the destination sites in Toms Cove. The route between Curtis Merritt and the NPS Visitor Center would offer the most direct water route to the public beach. Map 14 indicates, and anecdotal evidence from local boaters confirms, that access into Toms Cove is feasible for an appropriately shallow-drafted boat operated by someone with good knowledge of the local waters. The Harbor location is the furthest from the Town's commercial district, but is close to two large campgrounds. Use of Curtis Merritt as a ferry landing would require the Town to address slip and parking lot capacity issues.

Figure 26. Curtis Merritt Harbor Slips.

Source: Volpe Center, photograph, July 2009.

The Town's municipal docks are on the Chincoteague Channel, straddling the old Route 175 bridge in the downtown area, on the west side of the island (Figure 27). The primary purposes of these docks are commercial fishing operations and public foot access to the riverfront. There is no existing suitable infrastructure for passenger vessels operations at this time, that is, appropriately angled ramp(s) and a

---

[35] http://www.chincoteague.com/cruises/index.html.

[36] www.a-npdc.org and http://www.deq.state.va.us/coastal/seasidewatertrail/trailmap.html

float for loading and unloading passengers. Provision of same would likely detract considerably from the facility's current uses.

This location has the advantage of being closest to several guest accommodations and to the downtown area. It also is served regularly by the Pony Express. It is the furthest by water to all three destination sites on Assateague Island.

Figure 27. Chincoteague Municipal Docks.

Source: Volpe Center, photograph, July 2009.

The East Side boat ramp is on the Assateague Channel, with access from East Side Drive. The Channel affords direct and very short access to the Lighthouse site, as well as direct access to the mouth of Toms Cove. Parking capacity is approximately 50-75 cars. The main use of this facility is the ramp provided for recreational boaters and paddlers and commercial kayak outfits (Figure 28).

Figure 28. East Side Boat Ramp.

Source: Volpe Center, photograph, July 2009.

2. Assateague Island public marine facilities

The Assateague Lighthouse Landing is on the north side of CNWR, on the Assateague Channel, and consists of a boat ramp, a fixed dock and a floating dock connected by a ramp (Figure 29). Vehicular access is via an unpaved road about ¼ mile long, starting from the Beach Road, roughly opposite the FWS Visitor Center. The unimproved parking lot has a capacity of approximately 25 cars. The float and dock would be well suited to service for a small passenger vessel bringing visitors to the Lighthouse and the Visitor Center. Bicyclists would have convenient access to the CNWR bike paths. The existing dock and float would have to be evaluated for accessibility. It appears that only minor improvements would be necessary.

Figure 29. Assateague Lighthouse Landing.

Source: Volpe Center, photograph, July 2009.

The NPS Visitor Center at Toms Cove is on the south side of the Beach Road is the only site that would afford the visitor direct, convenient access to the public beach. An examination of the area along the boardwalk between the Visitor Center and the beach parking area (Figure 30) revealed no existing boat landing infrastructure and very shallow water in Little Toms Cove (ASIS staff stated that conditions at times restrict even kayak use).

Figure 30. NPS Visitor Center, Toms Cove.

Source: Volpe Center, photograph, July 2009.

The former U.S. Coast Guard Station lies on the west side of Toms Cove, within Toms Cove Hook. The Station is not connected by road to the rest of ASIS and CNWR and is only accessible by boat. There is existing, aging fixed dock infrastructure whose exact configuration and condition are not known to the project team (Figure 31). ASIS staff indicate that they view this site as one with great potential as an educational and cultural destination in the future. The access over the water appears to be suitable, via a small channel into Toms Cove from the Assateague Channel and through sufficiently deep water inside Toms Cove.

Figure 31. Former U.S. Coast Guard Station (Toms Cove).

Source: CNWR, photograph, credit: Brian Richardson, November 2009.

Intelligent Transportation Systems and Emergency Response

Intelligent Transportation Systems (ITS), as defined by US DOT RITA, "encompass a broad range of wireless and wire line communications-based information and electronics technologies" that "when integrated into the transportation system's infrastructure, and in vehicles themselves relieve congestion, improve safety and enhance American productivity." Emergency management, traffic management, and traveler information are three areas in which ITS solutions are commonly deployed in combination with other planning, preparedness, and response strategies.

VDOT has an extensive network of traffic cameras, variable message signs, and other ITS systems used for traffic and emergency management and traveler information that do not yet extend to Virginia's Eastern Shore. Thus, most of the existing management and response systems in the study area are provided locally, with state coordination only in response to major hurricane activity. This section describes the current existing ITS and emergency response systems in place for CNWR, the Town, and the State, and also describes the response to Hurricane Bill during the summer of 2009 as an example of the potential for ITS and other transportation interventions to help assist in emergency preparedness and response.

Existing CNWR/ASIS ITS and Emergency Resources

CNWR, in partnership with ASIS, has several systems set up and planned for emergencies. The ASIS 2009 Hurricane Plan, one of the Seashore's Emergency Operations Preparedness Plans, acknowledges the risks from hurricanes that the Seashore faces and outlines an "action plan" for both pre-storm and during the storm's development. The Plan, which is reviewed annually, is "designed to protect human life and property while at the same time attempting minimal disruption of visitor access to the island." ASIS is the lead agency in the document but coordinates with others, including CNWR. The Plan's appendices including the following:

- NPS Incident Command Organization

- USFWS Incident Command Organization-Major Response

- USFWS Incident Command Organization-Minor Response

- Town of Chincoteague Standard Operating Procedure for Chincoteague Causeway Closure

In October 2009, CNWR purchased a solar-powered, portable variable message sign (VMS) for use to inform visitors of CNWR and ASIS conditions, in particular during storm events and parking lot closures. The purchase was made after CNWR rented a VMS for use during the summer. CNWR has a designated AM frequency that is not currently operating or programmed. However, CNWR received a Federal Transit Administration grant to develop and implement a variety of ITS (detailed in Chapter 3).

Town Emergency Services

The Town of Chincoteague has an emergency operations plan and an emergency notification calling system (Reverse 911). The notification system enables the Town to call residents to inform them about emergency or important information such as utility outages, weather advisories, or possible evacuations. The Town currently uses a Verizon database that contains home numbers, business numbers, unlisted numbers, and unpublished numbers. People may add their cellular phone number to the database by submitting a form.37

The Town's government includes the following emergency response functions:

- Local Emergency Manager, who is part of the Virginia Department of Emergency Management's network of designated emergency management coordinators.

- Police Department 24-hour Communication Center, which operates the Chincoteague 911 Center and provides services to citizens, police, fire and rescue. The Center, by agreement with DOI, also provides dispatch services for the CNWR and ASIS.

In addition, the following two entities provide additional emergency services:

- Chincoteague Volunteer Fire Company, Inc. provides search and rescue services for both the Town of Chincoteague and ASIS and CNWR.

- The U.S. Coast Guard provides search and rescue services for water-related emergency events and is responsible for marine safety, environmental protection, and pollution response regulations and compliance.

Hurricane and Storm Activity

According to the Chincoteague *Comprehensive Plan* (2009), hurricanes and northeast storms are the two types of storms that impact the area. Hurricanes are a threat from May through November and on average, a tropical storm of hurricane force passes within 250 miles of Chincoteague once a year. Both hurricanes and nor'easters cause damage from winds and tidal surge. Due to overwash, storms can close roads and the beach parking lots on Assateague Island and the Route 175 Causeway.

The November 2009 storm event was of historical significance and caused the worst sustained flooding and damage to CNWR roads and infrastructure since 1992. It was a result of a nor'easter storm that arose from the remnants of Hurricane Ida and a low-pressure system.

Map 16 illustrates the area's historic vulnerability, showing the paths of the five most destructive and deadliest hurricanes affecting Virginia in modern times, including Hurricane Floyd (September 1999) and Hurricane Isabel (September 2003). All of the Virginia Eastern Shore, including Chincoteague and Assateague Islands, is designated as hurricane risk jurisdiction and at risk for storm surge. Map 17 shows the regions at risk by category of hurricane.

The U.S. Army Corps of Engineers conducted a study of Delmarva in 2006 that included an analysis of the potential tidal flooding from hurricanes based on storm surge heights calculated by the National

---

[37] Town of Chincoteague website. http://www.chincoteague-va.gov/

Weather Service's SLOSH (Sea, Lake, and Overland Surge from Hurricanes) Model. The analysis found that storm surge heights may range from 6.7 feet to 17.4 feet for Category 1 and 4 storms, respectively.

Evacuation

U.S. Route 13 is the designated hurricane evacuation route for the VA Eastern Shore. Due to wind restrictions, the Chesapeake Bay Bridge Tunnel is not a designated evacuation route. According to the *Virginia Hurricane Response Plan* (2009), evacuation clearance times for Accomack County and the Town of Chincoteague in a Category 4 storm would take up to 37 and 66 hours in low seasonal and high seasonal occupancy scenarios, respectively. It is noteworthy that for Category 3 and 4 storms, the evacuation times improve only 10 to 15 percent between slow and rapid responses.

Map 16. Storm Tracks, Five Worst Modern Tropical Storms in Region.

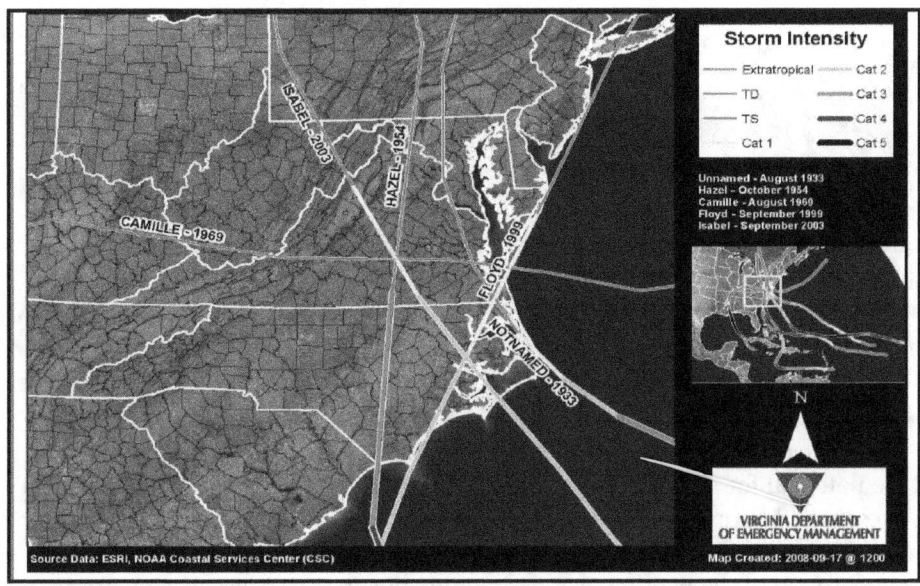

Source: Virginia Department of Emergency Management.

Map 17. Regional Storm Surge.

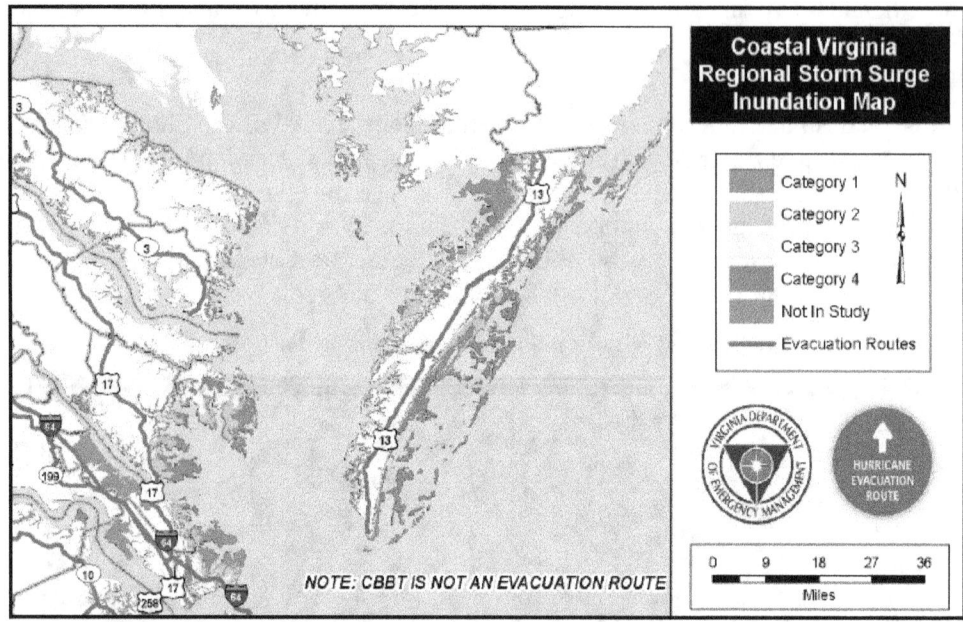

Source: 2008 Virginia Hurricane Evacuation Study.
http://www.vaemergency.com/library/plans/hurrplan/09_hurricane_respons_plan/Basic%20Plan%20Appendix%20III%20-%20June%202009.pdf.

Use of ITS during Hurricanes Bill and Danny, 2009

During August 2009, the preparations and response of CNWR, ASIS, and the Town to Hurricane Bill demonstrated the potential for coordination and deployment of ITS features. Hurricane Bill's course brought it within several hundred miles of Assateague Island during the weekend of August 22-23. A joint conference call on August 20 addressed potential impacts and concerns including visitor safety, high surf and waves, overwash of the parking lots, parking lot closures, and loss of temporary facilities/structures. The group addressed alternative transportation for beachgoers but no action was taken due to concerns about regulation of the Pony Express and deployment logistics on short notice.

To facilitate communication to the public, CNWR rented a variable message sign (VMS) and installed it on Beach Road at the entrance to CNWR and ASIS near the traffic circle (Figure 32). This location allowed visitors to read the swimming safety and beach parking lot condition statements before they arrived at the fee booths thus providing them the opportunity to turn around before paying the entrance fee. The VMS was again rented and used the following weekend for Tropical Storm Danny (Figure 33).

Figure 32. Location of VMS during Hurricane Bill.

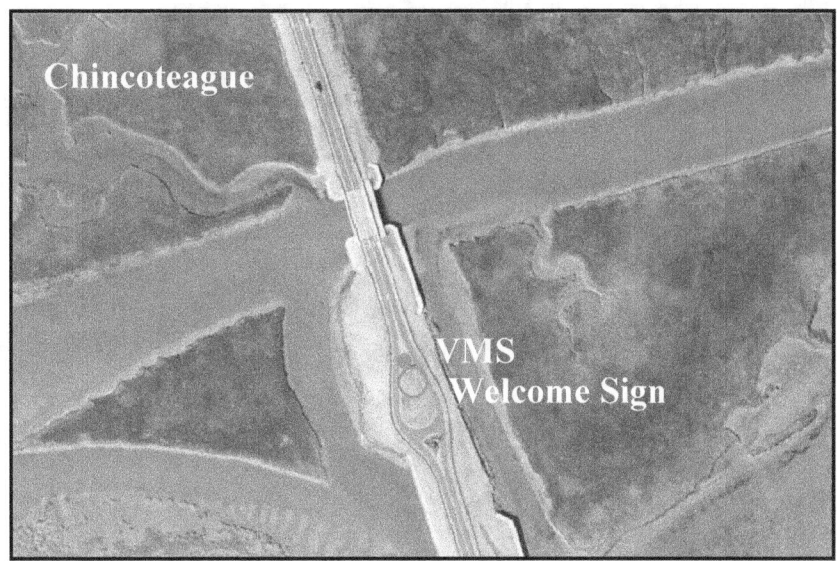

Source: Google Earth image with modifications by the Volpe Center.

Figure 33. VMS Location During Tropical Storm Danny.

Source: CNWR staff.

In addition to the VMS, the Refuge Manager also solicited the assistance of the local radio station, WCTG.FM, 96.5, to provide live updates on beach/parking conditions. The station general manager and program director conducted three live interviews with the Refuge Manager on Saturday and a fourth on Sunday. The public reaction was significant with non-stop calls to the radio station after the first broadcast asking for more information. In addition, people stopped by the radio station in person to ask for updates.

The experience with Hurricane Bill led CNWR to identify several next steps, including:

- CNWR should pursue the option of purchasing a VMS that can be programmed and managed by CNWR (as noted, CNWR purchased a portable VMS in October 2009)

- A process for deploying alternative transportation to the beaches should be identified and established

- The relationship between WCTG and CNWR should be strengthened and developed further so that emergency information can be broadcast to the public as rapidly as possible at a predetermined, preannounced time and so that call-ins from the public may be addressed on air

- CNWR should pursue the installation and programming of its AM Traveler Information Radio System to carry nonstop real-time information to the visiting public

3 Related Plans and Analyses

CNWR/ASIS

Impact of Climate Change on Infrastructure

The potential effects of climate change on Assateague Island and the Virginia Eastern Shore are an important concern of CNWR management, and the potential impact on transportation infrastructure is a key consideration in transportation planning. Understanding the environmental context of the transportation network can result in improved transportation facilities and operations that are better able to protect adjacent natural resources and be maintained and sustained over the long term.

The relevant work on climate change for the study area includes:

- *National Parks in Peril:The Threats of Climate Change Disruption*[38] identifies 25 national parks, including ASIS, as most at risk to climate change impacts. The report recommends that parks focus on reducing emissions of NPS operations and visitor activities, in particular due to transportation, through demonstrating model programs and becoming climate-neutral.
- *Sea Level Rise and Coastal Habitats in the Chesapeake Bay Region*[39] used the Sea Level Affecting Marshes Model (SLAMM)[40] to predict coastal changes, including impacts on coastal wildlife habitats, in the Chesapeake Bay region over the 21st century. The report notes that because of its expansive coastline, low-lying topography, and growing coastal population, the Chesapeake Bay region is one of the most vulnerable places in the nation to the impacts of sea-level rise. Many places along the Chesapeake Bay have seen a one-foot increase in relative sea-level rise over the 20th century, including six inches due to global warming and six inches due to naturally subsiding coastal lands. In looking at the Chesapeake Bay area, the report concluded that there would be significant inundation of dry-land and conversion to marshes by 2100 (see Map 18).

---

[38] Rocky Mountain Climate Organization and the Natural Resources Defense Council, "• National Parks in Peril: The Threats of Climate Change Disruption", 2009.

[39] National Wildlife Federation, "Sea Level Rise and Coastal Habitats in the Chesapeake Bay Region", 2008.

[40] SLAMM is one of the models used to study the impact of coastal processes, such as sea-level rise, on an area and simulate the dominant processes and forecast long-term effects. SLAMM takes into account five processes that determine the impact of sea level rise impact on wetlands: inundation: (the rise of water levels and the salt boundary); erosion; overwash (beach migration and transport of sediments); saturation (migration of coastal swamps and fresh marshes onto adjacent uplands due to the water table responding to rising sea level); and accretion (vertical rise due to buildup of organic and inorganic matter).

Map 18. SLAMM Analysis for Assateague and Chincoteague Islands.

Initial Condition (ca. 1990) vs. Year 2100, assuming 1 meter of global sea-level rise with developed land protected.

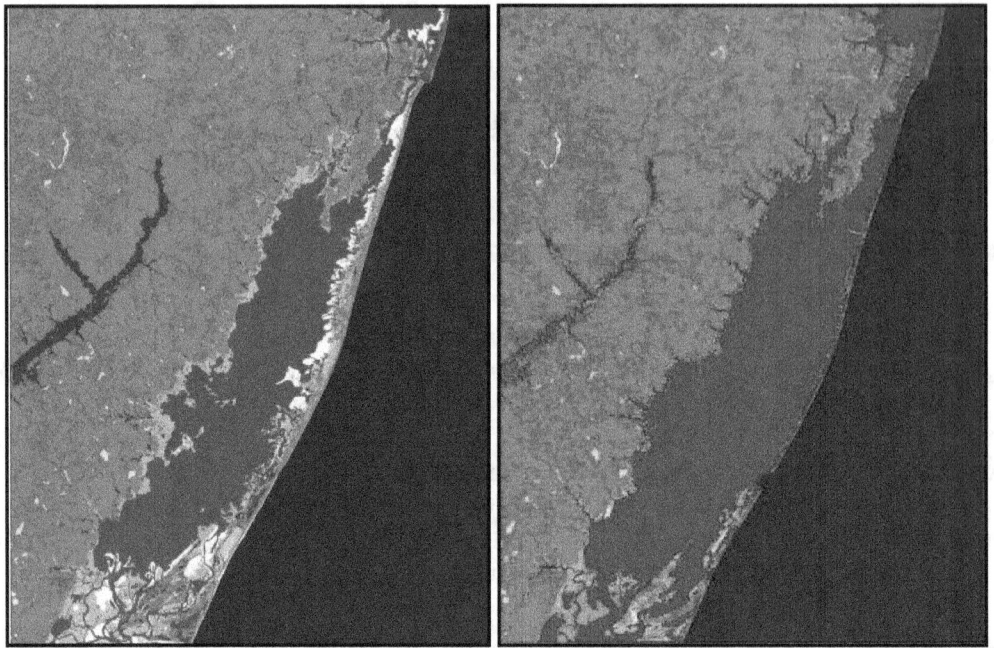

Source: *Sea Level Rise and Coastal Habitats in the Chesapeake Bay Region* (National Wildlife Federation).

- *Application of the Sea-Level Affecting Marshes Model (SLAMM 5.0.2) in the Lower Delmarva Peninsula* [41] was commissioned by CNWR to project the effects of sea-level rise on barrier islands extending from Ocean City Inlet, Maryland to Fisherman Island, Virginia in the Delmarva Peninsula with a main focus on CNWR and ASIS. The study used three scenarios:

  - International Panel on Climate Change (IPCC) A1B scenario: 0.7 meter global sea-level rise by 2100
  - 1.0 meter global sea level rise by 2100
  - 1.5 meter global sea level rise by 2100

Simulations were executed in 25 year increments from the date of available existing conditions (1988-2003) until 2100. The study found that the most significant changes would occur on the eastern shore beaches and marches. Breaching is expected along areas near Toms Cove and significant loss of coastal habitats is anticipated for Assateague Island and other barrier islands within CNWR by 2075 or 2100 in the 1.0 and 1.5 meter rise scenarios, respectively. Ocean beach habitat would decline by 80 percent by the year 2100 in the 1.0 meter sea-level rise scenario. Estuarine beaches, on the other hand, are projected to gain habitat. As with all ecological models, SLAMM does not currently account for all of the feedback and functions of coastal ecosystems.

The study indicates that critical transportation infrastructure is under threat of overwashes and inundation in the future, including the Route 175 Causeway, the bridge and causeway between Chincoteague and Assateague Islands, and low-lying stretches of Beach Road. As noted in the

---

[41] Nieves, Delissa Padilla. Application of the Sea-Level Affecting Marshes Model (SLAMM 5.0.2) in the Lower Delmarva Peninsula (Northampton and Accomack counties, VA / Somerset and Worcester counties, MD). National Wildlife Refuge System Conservation Biology Program. Arlington, VA. August 26, 2009.

CNWR *Master Plan*, the land now beneath current beach parking areas will eventually be reduced due to the natural movement of the barrier island, a movement that would most likely be exacerbated and added to by effects of climate change.

- *The Virginia Climate Change Action Plan*[42], published in 2008 by the Governor's Commission on Climate Change, identified sea level rise as a major concern for coastal Virginia. The Plan adopts the projections that sea levels in the Chesapeake Bay region will be 0.7-1.6 meters (2.3-5.2 feet) higher by 2100, reflecting those scenarios used in the SLAMM analyses, with great local variability as a result of subsidence. The Plan recommends that local governments in coastal Virginia and the Secretary of Transportation include projected climate change impacts, especially sea level rise and storm surge, in all planning efforts, including transportation planning, project design, and prioritization of projects for funding as well as transportation systems management, operations, and maintenance.

- *Refuges at Risk: the Threat of Global Warming*, a 2006 report by the Defenders of Wildlife, warns of the threat of global warming to National Wildlife Refuges and details its potential effects on ten national wildlife refuges that it considers the most endangered. Chincoteague NWR is included in the ten. The report states that scientists predict that Assateague Island will narrow due to sea-level rise leading to a loss in wildlife habitat and impacts to roads and visitor facilities.

- *A Case Study on Chesapeake Bay and Assateague Island*[43], part of the 2001 Climate Change, Wildlife, and Wildlands Toolkit by the U.S. Environmental Protection Agency in partnership with NPS and FWS, recognized the constant change in the shape and geographical position of Assateague Island and predicted that the island is likely to continue to move landward, as sand is pushed across the island to the bay side. It finds that similar habitats will probably not suffer serious net losses, but that infrastructure such as the Wildlife Loop Road may be destroyed.

Pedestrian/Bicycle Trail Extension (ATPPL Implementation Grant)

CNWR received a FY08 implementation project grant for $600,000 from the FTA's Paul S. Sarbanes Transit in the Parks Program to extend the existing pedestrian/bicycle path a quarter-mile from the bridge between Chincoteague and Assateague Islands to the Maddox Boulevard traffic circle (Figure 34). One-tenth mile of the path will be on NPS property and the remaining 0.15 mile will pass in front of four hotels and one campground within the Town of Chincoteague. This project will result in safer conditions for all users and improve connectivity between the Town and CNWR. The funding will cover design, construction, and National Environmental Policy Act (NEPA) compliance work. CNWR and ASIS have also applied for funding to extend the bicycle path along Beach Road to the beach.

---

[42] Governor's Commission on Climate Change. Final Report: A Climate Change Action Plan. December 15, 2008
http://www.deq.state.va.us/export/sites/default/info/documents/climate/CCC_Final_Report-Final_12152008.pdf

[43] http://www.epa.gov/climatechange/wycd/downloads/CS_Ches.pdf

Figure 34. Section of Maddox Boulevard Proposed for Bicycle/Pedestrian Trail Extension.

Source: ATTPL FY08 Implementation Project Application: Construct Pedestrian/Bike Trail

Intelligent Information Traffic Systems (ATPPL Implementation Grant)

CNWR received a second FY08 Transit in the Parks implementation project grant, for $350,000 to develop and implement a variety of intelligent information traffic systems, including the following:

- FM and/or AM radio Traveler Information Station capabilities
- Fee pass and information kiosks in hotels and public places
- Electronic informational signage

The project's purpose is to use these systems to inform the public of current traffic conditions and visitation alternatives, thus easing traffic congestion and improving safety by dispersing peak visitation traffic. The systems would:

- Inform the public of peak visitation times and of alternative modes by which to access CNWR (e.g., bicycling)
- Provide real-time information regarding parking availability, traffic congestion, and expected delays at CNWR and ASIS
- Provide off-site entrance fee purchase locations

FWS Intelligent Transportation Systems Demonstration Project

FWS is working with Eastern Federal Lands (EFL), a division of the Federal Highway Administration's Office of Federal Lands Highway, to conduct a national inventory of intelligent transportation systems on refuges and to conduct planning (Phase I) and implementation (Phase II) at several refuges. CNWR has been identified as a potential site, in part because of its needs, visitation, and geography, but also because of the ATPPL implementation grant it received. EFL has hired the consultant company Kimley-Horn and Associates to conduct the work and an initial meeting was held at CNWR in November 2009.

Town of Chincoteague

Comprehensive Plan (2009)

The Town's *Comprehensive Plan*, finalized in November 2009, is a result of a public process that began in 2003 with a visioning workshop and public workshops, followed by additional stakeholder meetings in 2007. The vision of the Plan is:

> "The Town of Chincoteague seeks to change over time in an economically and environmentally sustainable manner so that it retains the most endearing and unique physical and cultural features of the Town and provides the setting for a harmonious community life."

The Plan specifies goals for land use, economic development, community facilities and services, transportation, and housing. The transportation goal and objectives are:

- Provide for the safe and efficient movement of people and goods.
  - Provide a safe and comfortable system of pedestrian and bicycle pathways;
  - Look at the possibility of having a downtown parking garage; and
  - Provide safe, efficient, reliable transportation for many modes of transportation.

In addition, the Plan describes a multi-modal approach for transportation that promotes sharing the road among drivers, pedestrians, and cyclists and includes the following objectives:

- Improve vehicular circulation by upgrading streets where feasible, requiring connectivity between adjacent properties and requiring new development to make improvements to the existing street system;
- Continue to provide and enhance local transit service; and
- Improve safety and convenience for pedestrians and bicyclists by planning and developing a community wide system of bike routes and pedestrian trails.

The Plan also describes the Town's goal to create a commercial corridor planning area for Maddox Boulevard and notes the importance of Maddox Boulevard as a gateway for visitors. It identifies the following purposes of the planning area:

- To concentrate highway oriented commercial uses along Maddox Boulevard;
- To enhance the visual image of this gateway corridor; and
- To ensure safe movement of vehicles and people.

Transportation-related implementation strategies for Maddox Boulevard include:

- Work with VDOT to enhance vehicular and pedestrian safety in the corridor;
- Seek State assistance to develop a "Corridor Management Plan" to identify opportunities to enhance access controls and assure the corridor can sustain adequate levels of service to accommodate projected future traffic volumes;
- Facilitate transit service in the corridor;
- Consider more off-street parking options especially for the businesses; and
- Implement the Town's bicycle plan.

Land use and transportation planning maps and a table of transportation recommendations from the Comprehensive Plan appear in Appendix C.

Bicycle Plan (2009)

The Town of Chincoteague has a bicycle transportation plan, originally completed in October 1997 by the Town's Public Works Committee with technical assistance from the Accomack-Northampton Planning

District Commission. It is intended to meet VDOT requirements for project funding.[44] The plan is currently being revised by the Recreation and Community Enhancement Committee. Updates to the plan during 2009 include a recommendation to disseminate the bicycle safety video completed in 2004 to schools and through the Town website and local access Cable TV and documentation of the "School Travel Plan," as required for the Safe Routes to School Program. The latter identifies and promotes solutions for children to walk and ride their bikes to school.

The Town applied for a grant from the Safe Routes to Schools program in fall 2008 to install pedestrian buttons and signals and pavement markings at signalized intersections (particularly on Maddox at Chicken City and Deep Hole) but the application was not successful.

The draft bicycle plan provides goals, trip origins and destinations, needs assessment, and recommendations. Goals and objectives focus on safety, access, facilities, and tourism and the recommended solutions include:

- Widening Chicken City Road, Eastside Road, portions of South and North Main Street, Bunting Road and Beebe Road to provide paved shoulders;
- Elimination of on-street parking on Church Street and portions of Maddox Boulevard;
- Striping as required; and
- Property acquisitions to build separate bicycle paths in places including along the waterfront parallel to Main Street.

Main Street Enhancement Project (2008)

The Town of Chincoteague received a Transportation Enhancement Grant and developed a streetscape master plan for Main Street from Cropper Street to Maddox Boulevard. The Town hired Land Studio PC to conduct a community design charette and develop a master plan. The consultant began work in December 2008, conducted the charette in January 2009, and finalized the master plan in February 2009 (Figure 35). Recommendations focused on parking and various streetscape elements, such as pavers, lighting, and trees. The Town does not currently have funds to construct the recommended improvements.

---

[44] Town of Chincoteague Public Works Committee, "Town of Chincoteague Bicycle Plan", draft, 2008.

Figure 35. Main Street Streetscape Master Plan.

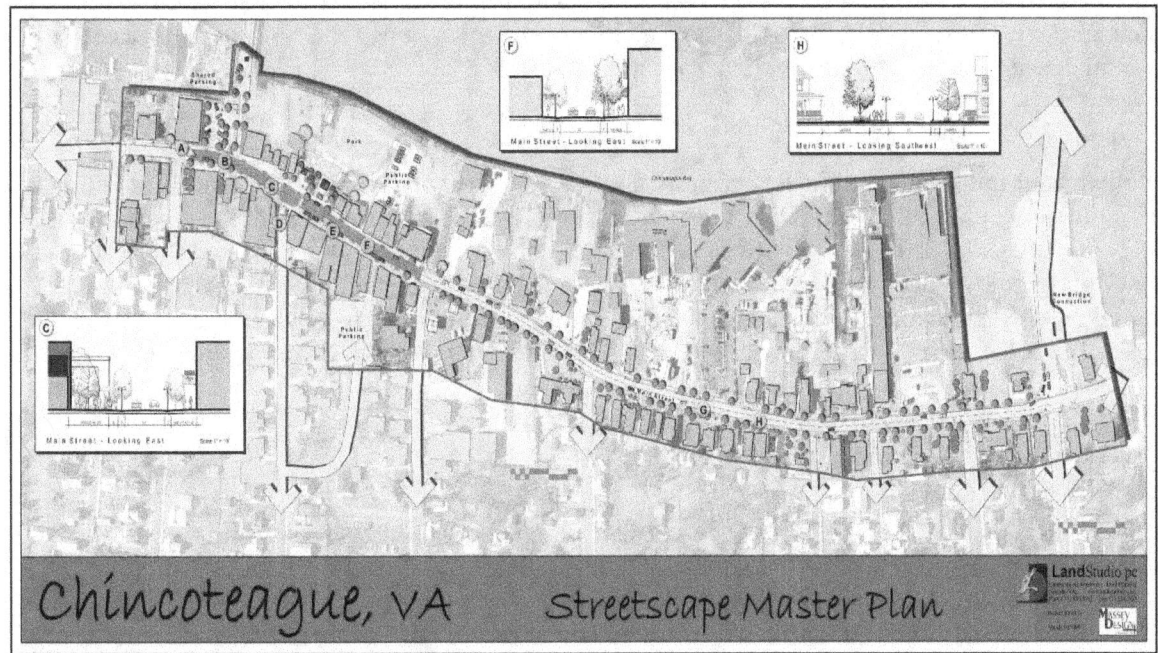

Source: Town of Chincoteague, prepared by Land Studio PC.

2020 Transportation Plan (2002)

The *Chincoteague 2020 Transportation Plan* was developed through the joint efforts of VDOT, the Town of Chincoteague, and Accomack County. The purpose of the study was to evaluate the transportation system in the Town of Chincoteague and to recommend transportation improvements. Recommendations include:

- Development of a Town trolley service (implemented in 2004);
- The addition of a bicycle lane and elimination of some street parking on Main Street and Maddox Boulevard; and
- Some reconstruction of selected roads and intersections to allow for bicycle facilities and sidewalks.

One of the Plan's recommendations, the realignment of the intersection of Chicken City Road and Ridge Road, is included in VDOT's FY10 *Six-Year Improvement Plan*. Planning and engineering is underway, with construction scheduled for 2012.[45]

Future Traffic Projections and Analyses

VDOT's *2025 State Highway Plan* (the Plan) was again consulted for estimates of future operating conditions on roadways in the Town of Chincoteague. The results included traffic projections on roadway sections and operating levels of service (LOS), which are detailed in Table 7.

Based on the results of VDOT's planning analysis, most roadways in the Town will continue to operate at acceptable levels of service. The two exceptions are Main Street and Maddox Boulevard. In particular, the section of Maddox Boulevard between Chicken City Road and the entrance to Assateague Island is

---

[45] Six-year Improvement Plan. http://syip.virginiadot.org/docs/FY10-FINAL-SYIP.pdf

projected to operate at Level of Service F in the year 2025. Widening the roadway is not a viable option due to the fact that the bridge into CNWR consists of only one travel lane in each direction. Reducing vehicle traffic and providing safe and efficient alternative travel options for CNWR will be necessary to accommodate any additional growth in visitation.

Route 175 Causeway Bridge

The only major transportation project currently under way in the study area is VDOT's construction of a new ¾ mile-long bridge between the Route 175 Causeway and Chincoteague, with alignment at Maddox Boulevard, almost half a mile north of where the current bridge connects to the island. The bridge will have 8-foot shoulders but no sidewalk or bicycle lanes. A new 729-foot connector bridge will also be built linking the new bridge to Marsh Island. The section of the new bridge over Lewis Creek Channel will be a drawbridge (see Map 19 and Figure 36). The construction contract was awarded in January of 2007 and the scheduled completion date for the new bridge is April 2010, with final demolition of old bridges occurring by June 2010.

Table 7. Projected Levels of Service, Town of Chincoteague Roads.

Facility Name	Segment From	Segment To	Flow Rate 2015	OLS 2015	Flow Rate 2025	OLS 2025
North Main Street	Route 175 Bridge	Church Street	642	C	846	D
North Main Street	Church Street	Maddox Blvd.	604	D	604	D
Ridge Road	Beebe Road	Bunting Road	195	B	212	B
Ridge Road	Bunting Road	Church Street	288	B	420	C
Chicken City Rd.	Church Street	Maddox Blvd.	357	A	502	A
Chicken City Rd.	Maddox Blvd.	Deep Hole Road	117	A	146	A
Church Street	Main Street	Willow Street	318	B	512	C
Church Street	Willow Street	Pension Street	385	C	537	C
Church Street	Pension Street	0.15 mi east of Pension	336	B	482	C
Deep Hole Road	Pension Street	Ocean Avenue	223	B	313	B
Deep Hole Road	Ocean Avenue	Maddox Blvd.	229	B	332	B
Deep Hole Road	Maddox Blvd.	Chicken City Rd.	196	B	269	B
Maddox Blvd.	Main Street	Deep Hole Road	528	B	851	B
Maddox Blvd.	Deep Hole Road	Chicken City Rd.	579	B	894	B
Maddox Blvd.	Chicken City Rd.	Entrance CNWR	879	C	1175	F

Source: VDOT Needs Analysis Traffic Forecasts, compiled by Volpe Center.

Map 19. Route 175 Bridge Construction Plan.

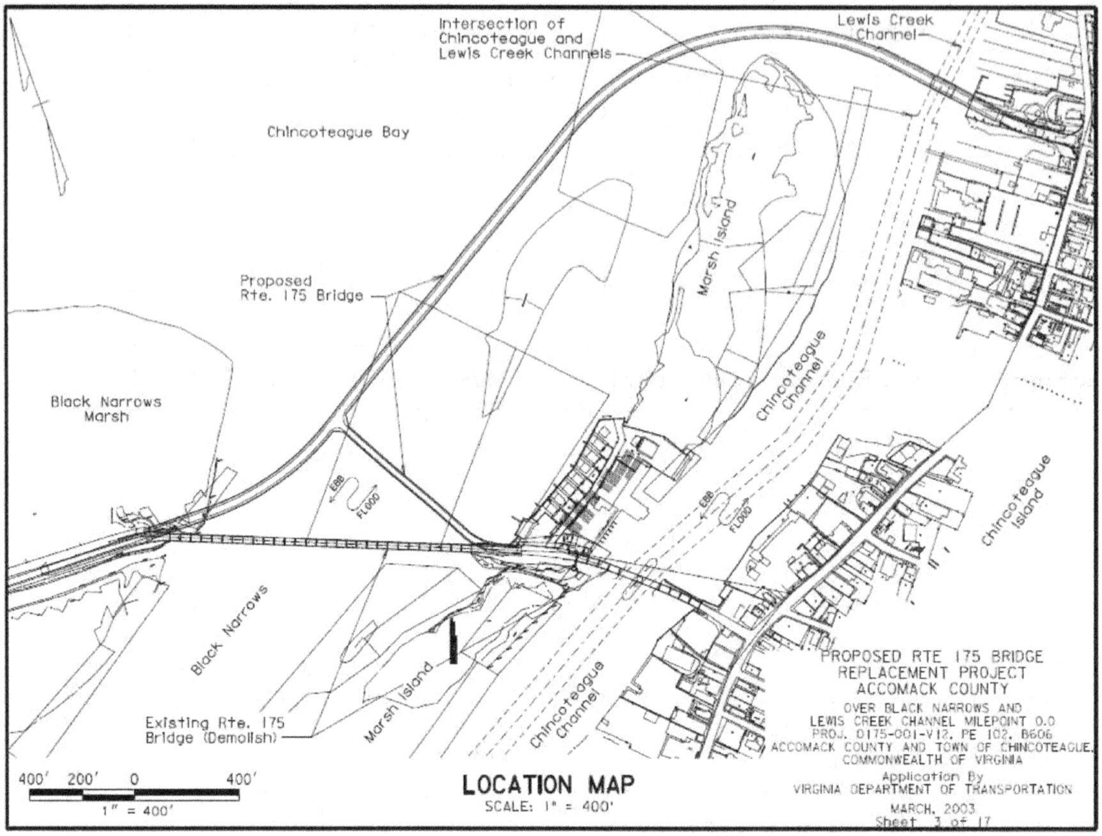

Source: Virginia DOT. http://www.virginiadot.org/images/projects/chincoteaguebrodgeallignment.jpg.

Figure 36. Route 175 Bridge Construction, Aerial Photo, January 2009.

Source: Virginia DOT. http://www.virginiadot.org/VDOT/Projects/Hampton_Roads/asset_upload_file747_22712.jpg.

VDOT lists the benefits of the bridge relocation as follows[46]:

- Reduces traffic congestion in downtown Chincoteague
- Allows boats better channel access
- Reduces the number of necessary bridge openings
- Increases safety by providing wider lanes and shoulders
- Improves industrial access by allowing VDOT to consider permits for overweight loads

In its new location, the bridge will align with Maddox Boulevard, almost one-half mile north of its current terminus just south of Church Street. A fully-actuated traffic signal is planned for the Main Street/Maddox Boulevard intersection. Due to the presence of historical properties, it was not possible to accommodate any widening for the Main Street or Maddox Boulevard approaches. As shown in Figure 37, the proposed intersection configuration includes two-lane approaches on the bridge approach and Main Street (exclusive left-turn and shared through/right lane) and a single lane approach on Maddox Boulevard. All four approaches include a left turn arrow signal which will allow vehicles to proceed in an advance phase with no opposing traffic. A crosswalk and pedestrian pushbutton and signal will be installed on the bridge approach.

The new bridge and alignment will change traffic circulation patterns in the Town of Chincoteague. VDOT's intersection capacity analyses provide details of peak hour traffic volumes, including 2010 and 2020 projections. However, the intersection configuration in the analyses is different than what is shown the final design plan; therefore, the results are not relevant. It is likely that VDOT will monitor traffic volumes after the signal is installed and adjust the signal to provide optimized operations for peak periods.

---

[46] http://www.virginiadot.org/projects/hamptonroads/chincoteague_bridge_replacement.asp

Figure 37. Route 175 Intersection Realignment.

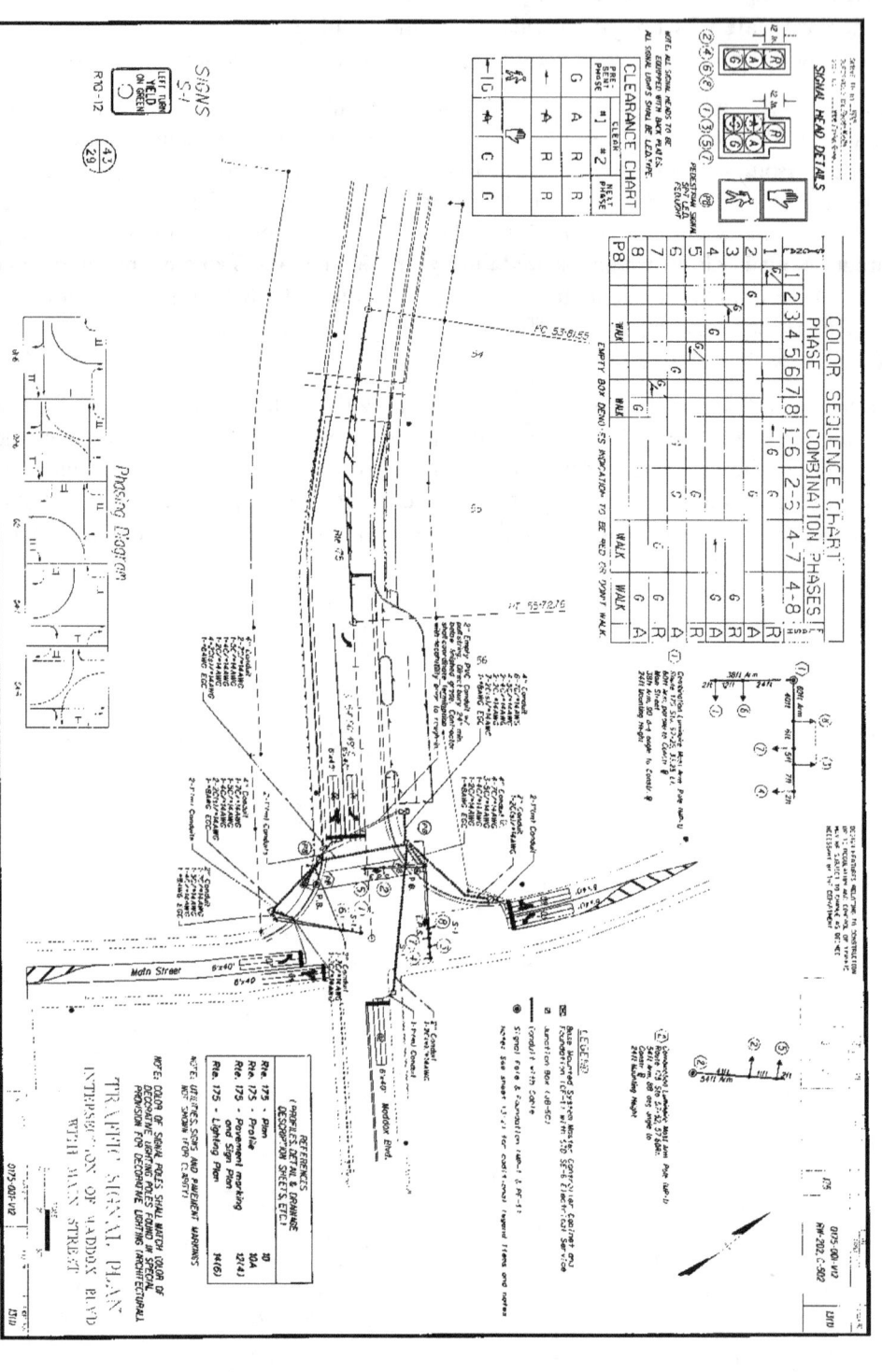

Source: Virginia DOT. http://www.virginiadot.org/images/projects/chincoteaguebrodgealignment.jpg.

70

The realignment will increase traffic along Maddox Boulevard between Main Street and Chicken City Road. In the bridge's existing configuration, travelers headed to CNWR turn left onto Main Street and then turn right onto Church Street or Maddox Boulevard. Although Maddox Boulevard is signed as the primary route to CNWR, drivers familiar with the area have the option of using Church Street and Chicken City Road as a bypass route. Increased volume along Maddox Boulevard will be especially difficult during seasonal peaks due to the high number of access drives for businesses along this section of road. Turning vehicles will block through traffic and vehicles exiting onto Maddox Boulevard will experience increased delays.

Traffic volumes will decrease in downtown Chincoteague on Main Street resulting in improved traffic operations during peak flows. This improvement is particularly significant given the proximity of the fire station to the existing bridge location.

Accomack County

Route 13 / Wallops Island Access Management Study (2002)

The Route 13 / Wallops Island Access Management Study, prepared for VDOT by a consultant,[47] made several recommendations that have not yet been implemented. The first was that Route 175, from Route 13 to Atlantic Road, be improved to include 12-foot shoulders, turn lanes, and localized widening. An alternative to this recommendation, construction of a new controlled-access, four-lane divided highway along the same section of road, was rejected. The study also recommended improvements at the intersection at Routes 13 and Route 175. The three alternatives considered are shown below in Figure 38 below.

Figure 38. Alternatives for Route 175 Intersection with U.S. Route 13.

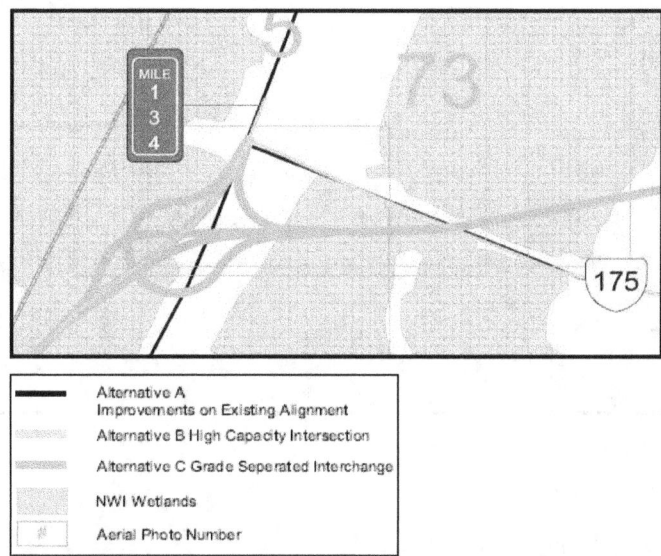

Source: Route 13/Wallops Island Access Management Study (VDOT).

Finally, the VDOT study recommended building 10-foot shoulders at a minimum along the entire length of Route 13 and maintaining the shoulders as passable and free from debris. This improvement is intended to provide safer conditions for vehicles entering and exiting driveways on Route 13 and to better

---

[47] Route 13 / Wallops Island Access Management Study. May 2002. Virginia Department of Transportation. http://virginiadot.org/projects/resources/hampton_roads/rte13_final_report.pdf

accommodate bicyclist and pedestrian travel. The road would still only be recommended for advanced or experienced bicyclists given the speed of traffic (45/55mph posted) and function of the corridor.

Eastern Shore of Virginia Bicycle Plan (2004)

The Eastern Shore of Virginia Bicycle Committee, with technical assistance from the Accomack-Northampton Planning District Commission, completed the *Eastern Shore of Virginia Bicycle Plan* in 2004 (Map 20). Similar to the Chincoteague bicycle plan, the *Eastern Shore of Virginia Bicycle Plan* was completed with the intention of fulfilling VDOT's planning requirement for bicycle facility funding. The Plan presents a vision that includes the following proposed facilities for its study area:

- Paved shoulders on Route 175 from Route 13 to the intersection with Route 679
- Paved shoulders on the Route 175 Causeway
- Improved access along and across Route 13, including a shared use path and a designated Seaside Bicycle Route using parallel routes
- Rail trail from Maryland to Cape Charles along the Eastern Shore Railroad right-of-way
- Shuttle bus service across the Chesapeake Bay Bridge Tunnel with bicycle capacity

Map 20. Eastern Shore of Virginia Bicycle Plan Map.

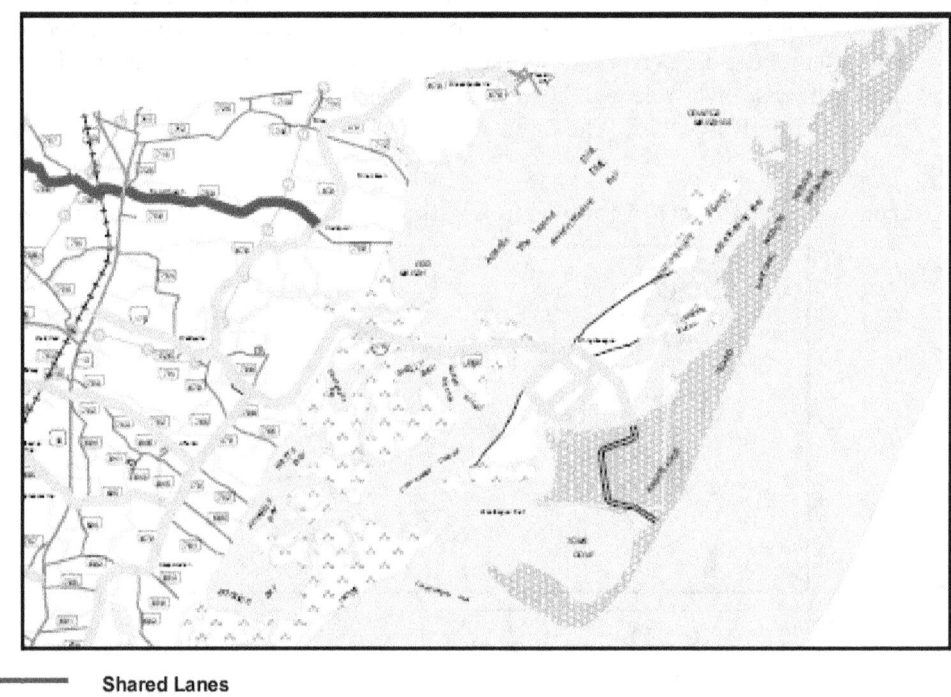

—————— **Shared Lanes**

·········· **Paved Shoulders**

Source: *Eastern Shore of Virginia Bicycle Plan*, 2004 .

Accomack County Comprehensive Plan

The Accomack County Comprehensive Plan (2008),[48] makes the following two recommendations in regard to the study area:

---

[48] Respecting the Past, Creating the Future: Accomack County Comprehensive Plan. May 14, 2008.
http://www.co.accomack.va.us/Planning/2008_comprehensive_plan_update.html

- "The USFWS should continue to work closely with the National Park Service and private partners to optimize compatible recreational opportunities at Chincoteague National Wildlife Refuge and Assateague Island National Seashore while protecting sensitive beach habitat."
- "Studies of Assateague Island National Seashore should be completed to determine where appropriate support facilities could be located while preserving the integrity of the bays, dune systems and vegetation. Development of a transit system and improved bicycle facilities to supplement vehicle access to the island's recreational resources should be considered."

2035 Rural Long-Range Transportation Plan[49]

The Virginia Department of Transportation (VDOT) and 20 planning district commissions throughout the Commonwealth of Virginia, including the Accomack-Northampton Planning District Commission, are partnering to evaluate the State's rural transportation system and to recommend a range of transportation improvements that best satisfy existing and future needs. The plan has a target completion date of March 2010. Once completed, the regional transportation plan will be incorporated into Virginia's *2035 State Highway Plan,* which is developed by VDOT to identify needs and recommend solutions for the Commonwealth's Interstate and primary highway systems. In turn, once completed, *the 2035 State Highway Plan* will serve as a key component to *VTrans2035*, Virginia's statewide long-range multimodal transportation plan. The Governor's Commission on Climate Change charged *VTrans2035* to include "a complete reevaluation of the state's transportation plans, capital investment programming, and projects in light of climate change, higher energy prices, and changing demographics."[50]

[49] http://virginiadot.org/projects/pdf/acco_nh.pdf and http://virginiadot.org/projects/rural_regional_long-range_plans.asp

[50] Governor's Commission on Climate Change. Final Report: A Climate Change Action Plan. December 15, 2008

http://www.deq.state.va.us/export/sites/default/info/documents/climate/CCC_Final_Report-Final_12152008.pdf

4 Outreach and Public Input

Public Involvement Strategy

This transportation study included the solicitation of information, experiences, ideas, and suggestions for transportation alternatives from the public and other stakeholders in the study area. The purposes of these outreach efforts were to inform the public about the transportation study, to provide an opportunity for stakeholders to provide input on their transportation concerns, and to facilitate the identification of potential alternatives for solutions. The main points of the outreach strategy were:

- A working group including CNWR, ASIS, and the FWS Northeast Region to address outreach and partnership opportunities
- Public outreach through other programs and opportunities managed by FWS and NPS, including the ASIS GMP
- Media outreach through print and electronic media
- Development and monitoring of e-mail and Web-based resources as avenues for providing public information and receiving public input.
- Facilitation of conference calls, public meetings, and interviews with partners and stakeholders

The focus of the outreach effort was stakeholders outside of the co-applicants and public and private partner entities. These included:

- Seasonal visitors such as beachgoers, hunters, and birders
- Seasonal residents
- Year-round residents
- Business owners

Public Meetings

The Volpe Center worked with CNWR and regional FWS staff to hold three public outreach events. The project team solicited attendance for these meetings through local media and radio announcements, print media, and announcements on the project website developed in cooperation with the FWS Northeast Region Office[51]. The public had access to the following documents posted on the project's website:

- "What is the Chincoteague Alternative Transportation Study?" background document
- Summary of results of the January 2008 TAG meeting
- Agendas and summaries for the October and January public meetings
- Maps of the study area, Town and CNWR, and shoreline change for Toms Cove

Public meetings targeting full-time and part-time residents were held in October 2008 and January 2009 and an outreach event for summer visitors was held in July 2009. The particulars of those meetings are described below and a summary of the concerns and ideas raised in these meetings appears in "Public Response Summary" at the end of the chapter.

October 2008 Public Meetings

Two public meetings were held in October 2008 at the Chincoteague Center, wherein the project team introduced the transportation study to an audience comprised primarily of full-time residents and CNWR and ASIS staff (Figure 39). The meetings featured presentations by the project team, small discussion or "break out" groups, and dialogue among all participants allowing an open forum to express both concerns and ideas on transportation.

---

[51] http://www.fws.gov/northeast/planning/Chincoteague/alternativetrans html.

Figure 39. Public Meeting at the Chincoteague Center, October 2008.

Source: Volpe Center photograph, October 2008.

The meetings were held at 9 am and 6 pm on Thursday, October 16th, in order to accommodate residents, business owners, and other stakeholders. Approximately 75 people participated in the two meetings, including the study co-applicants and members of the project team, full-time/year-round residents, seasonal residents, business owners, local community leaders, and elected officials including Chincoteague Mayor Jack Tarr and Accomack County Supervisor Wanda Thornton. Sylvia Parks of U.S. Representative Thelma Drake's district office also attended. Fifteen staff members from the National Park Service and Fish and Wildlife Service participated.

At the start of each meeting, attendees were asked to share one word that describes transportation on Chincoteague. Their responses showed a wide spectrum of opinion and experience: sparse, parking, changing, slow, needed/necessity, enjoyable, pedestrians, compatible, chaotic, mopeds, a privilege, easy-going, un-stressful, dangerous, seasonal, simple, funding, lost tourists, congested, bicycles, the bridge.

After brief presentations by the Volpe Center, CNWR staff, and elected officials, including the results of the January 2008 Transportation Assistance Group (TAG) workshop, participants went into break-out groups for discussion and were asked to consider two questions:

> (1) What do you see as the major transportation concerns at CNWR, at the beach, and in Chincoteague?

> (2) What are your ideas for possible solutions?

The responses are incorporated in the "Public Response Summary", section 4-e.

January 2009 Public Meeting

The third public meeting was held in January, also at the Chincoteague Center, using a similar format. This meeting began at 2 pm on Saturday, January 17, to accommodate second-home owners, visitors, business owners, and other stakeholders with commitments during the week. Approximately 20 people participated in the meeting, including a Town Council member and several residents who attended the October meetings. The Volpe Center team again conducted the meeting, and project co-applicants attended, including Chincoteague Mayor Jack Tarr, Accomack County Supervisor Wanda Thornton, and FWS and NPS staff.

Again, brief presentations by the Volpe Center, CNWR staff, and elected officials preceded discussion in break out groups. Attendees were provided with summaries of the October 2008 public meetings and the January 2008 TAG workshop and were asked to assess the strengths, weaknesses, opportunities, and threats relative to the transportation system.

The responses are incorporated in the "Public Response Summary", section 4-e.

Pony Swim, July 2009

The project team and CNWR staff organized a public outreach event held on July 27, 2009 during the week of the Annual Pony Swim and Auction. The effort took place from 6 am-2:30 pm on Monday, July 27, under a tent adjacent to the pony corrals near Beach Road in CNWR (Figure 40). The tent featured six posters, comment postcards, and paper and markers for immediate comments. Three Volpe Center staff and the Refuge Manager, Lou Hinds, were on hand to introduce the study, answer questions, and solicit comments.

This event succeeded in engaging hundreds of visitors who came to view the ponies. The project team and Mr. Hinds engaged summer visitors and solicited their comments and ideas on transportation to and around the study area (Figure 41). Overall, the summer visitors said they were pleased with their transportation experiences and in particular enjoyed the bicycle trails. Respondents expressed interest in extending and improving the bicycle facilities, especially from the terminus of the existing trail to the beach and in the Town, and in transit options, including the extension of the Pony Express to stops within CNWR and use of alternative fuel vehicles. These responses are incorporated in the "Public Response Summary", section 4-e.

Figure 40. Public Outreach Event Tent at the Pony Corrals, July 2009.

Source: Volpe Center photograph, July 2009.

Figure 41. Lou Hinds, CNWR Refuge Manager, Speaking with Visitors at the Pony Penning, July 2009.

Source: Volpe Center photograph, July 2009.

ASIS General Management Plan Outreach

ASIS and NPS Regional staff solicited comments from the public about transportation to and from Assateague Island during public outreach activities in July and August 2009, in the ASIS Maryland and Virginia Districts, and in September 2009 at local community centers, in support of the development of the ASIS General Management Plan (GMP). The public was asked to respond to the question: "How can we make it easier to get onto and around the Seashore?"

The ASIS GMP team received 118 responses to this question. For these purposes, this study addresses only those comments collected within the Virginia District for Chincoteague (58 responses or 49 percent of the total), which includes CNWR. In summary, nearly half of the comments indicated that no change is necessary. Of the rest, some felt that access could be improved, but did not offer specific suggestions, and there was a strong showing of people recommending added transit from Chincoteague to ASIS and to access other parts of Assateague Island. In descending order of numerical responses, others suggested bicycle access improvements, namely extending and improving the separated trail; adding an express lane to the entrance booths for people with passes; improved provision of and access for small motorized vehicles spreading visitation geographically over CNWR; and improved wayfinding and signage on the approaches to Chincoteague and CNWR.

These responses are incorporated in the "Public Response Summary", section 4-e.

Written Comments

The outreach effort included two methods for soliciting written information: an email address (chincoteagueplanning@dot.gov) for electronic submissions and a postcard developed for submission of comments by mail.

Commenters submitted eleven emails, eight postcards, and one written letter. Of these 20 submissions, two commenters participated in at least one of the public meetings. The comments came primarily from local year-round or summer residents, home-owners and long-time visitors. These responses are incorporated in the "Public Response Summary", section 4-e.

Public Response Summary

The observations, concerns and issues, and solutions and ideas captured in the public outreach process were, in part, the basis for the development of transportation solutions and alternatives addressed in Chapters 6 and 7. Some ideas were not included because they fell outside the scope of the study, were cost prohibitive, or were in direct opposition to the mission and management decisions of CNWR and ASIS. Chapter 6 includes explanations for the exclusion of transportation-related ideas.

Observations

Comments from public meeting participants and written submissions consistently lauded the unique nature of Assateague Island, in particular its natural beach and other natural amenities, its status as a national resource, and its balance between preservation of nature and access to nature. Many commenters recognized that this balance can give rise to conflict among the various missions and interests of CNWR, ASIS, and Town, all of which serve a great variety of visitor interests and access needs. A number of participants responded to questions about the future by expressing their desire for everything to stay the same, particularly in regard to retaining and maintaining the current level of beach parking and access. Finally, some participants acknowledged concern about the impact of the new bridge on future traffic.

Concerns and Issues

The major concerns and issues identified in the outreach process fall into the following themes: safety, traffic congestion, vehicular access (including access for the mobility impaired), and quality of the visitor experience.

1. Safety and Emergency Vehicle Access

Safety was a top concern, in particular:

- Bicycling safety. Participants noted that Town and CNWR roads provide inadequate separation for bicyclists from vehicle traffic, and have narrow or nonexistent shoulders or bike lanes and rough surfaces. Cyclists are often inexperienced and include young children who are either unaccompanied or inadequately supervised. Several also mentioned the inadequacy of sidewalks on major roads in the Town.
- Shared road use. Participants expressed concern about the shared use of roads by multiple modes, including the various non-motorized and small motorized vehicles that can be rented in Chincoteague.
- Route 175 Causeway. Participants expressed concern about roadway width for vehicular and bicycle safety, as well as emergency vehicle access.
- Emergency shelter, evacuation and response. Participants were concerned about emergency vehicle access to the beach, evacuation from the beach, and shelter at the beach.

2. Traffic Congestion

Participants generally agreed that traffic congestion is experienced during a short period in the summertime, primarily during July and August, holiday weekends, and the Pony Penning week. Backups are concentrated at the CNWR entrance booths, resulting in traffic queues and long wait times for travelers going to the beach.

3. Vehicular Access

There was a strong assertion by many participants that vehicle access to the beach, including parking, should be maintained as is. Even supporters of public transportation alternatives acknowledged the importance of maintaining some automobile access into CNWR. A few suggested maintaining automobile access for nature-oriented activities and sites only.

Participants identified a number of barriers to public transportation and reasons for maintaining automobile access, including:

- Transporting gear (coolers, chairs, etc.) to the beach requires a car;
- Many popular activities at CNWR (beach volleyball, kayaking, surf fishing) require the transportation of equipment;
- The primary mode for beach access for the mobility-impaired is private vehicles and parking at the existing beach lots;
- Family access to beach is important and is seen as incompatible with public transit;
- Visitor experience and perception of Chincoteague and Assateague Islands as a destination is dependent on a positive experience with direct, convenient access to the beach; and,
- Safe evacuation and sheltering of visitors may be difficult to implement when using transit.

4. Quality of Visitor Experience

Some participants raised a variety of concerns about negative impacts on natural and historic resources and the prospect of exacerbation due to increased visitation, including the following:

- Litter;
- Noise levels produced by vehicles accessing CNWR; and
- Undesirable changes to the town character of Chincoteague and the natural character of Assateague.

Solutions and Ideas

Participants and commenters offered many solutions and ideas, which are organized thematically as: traveler information, CNWR entrance, beach parking, bicycle and pedestrian access, public transportation, emergency access, handicapped access, and other. Many participants emphasized the need for agency collaboration and regional perspective, provision of multiple options to match the needs of the various users, positive consideration of Chincoteague as a gateway community, and examination of solutions used elsewhere.

1. Traveler Information

Commenters recommended the provision of pre-trip planning information, real-time parking and traffic information, educational guidance on bicycle etiquette, and wayfinding improvements such as better signage and maps.

2. CNWR Entrance

The focus of comments on the CNWR entrance was on the provision of a separate designated lane for pass holders and transit, an automated pass-reader system, and off-site and online pass sales.

3. Beach Parking

There was a diversity of responses in the matter of beach parking, because of the desire to retain its convenience in its current form and the realization by some that the beach lots may not be sustainable due to shoreline change. A couple of participants expressed concern about the costs associated with investing in facilities that need to be repeatedly rebuilt such as the parking areas and Swan Cove trail. Others felt that the current lot capacity should be maintained by sand replenishment, snow fencing, and other erosion prevention strategies; some felt that parking capacity should be increased; and still others felt it should be decreased.

Some participants considered the possibility of creating a new bay beach or moving the beach area and parking further north. In this scenario, the new northern location accessed via the service road or via Wildlife Loop would supplement the existing lots as they are diminished. Access to the Toms Cove area would still be maintained for certain uses (fishing, hiking, and birding).

4. Bicycle and Pedestrian Access

All participants were generally interested in the extension and improvement of bicycle facilities, especially from the Town to CNWR, from the terminus of the existing trail to the beach, and within the Town. Participants were also interested in sidewalk improvements within the Town, especially along Main Street and Maddox Boulevard.

5. Public Transportation

Several participants identified improved or new transit service features, in particular service from off-site parking and other sites to the beach and other CNWR destinations, as desirable. There were suggestions to widen the Beach Road access bridge to allow transit vehicles to bypass any traffic back-ups at the entrance booths, to expand transit service within CNWR, and to use alternative fuel vehicles. A few comments proposed the elimination of all vehicles except transit from certain Town roads and from CNWR. However, many participants identified the practical barriers to implementation of public transit, feeling that it should an option rather than the exclusive means of access to CNWR, and that there should at least be exceptions or strategies for certain users.

6. Safety and Emergency Vehicle Access

Recommendations for improvement on the Route 175 Causeway included eliminating passing zones, adding shoulders and emergency pull-off areas, and increasing enforcement of speed limits.

For the Beach Road bridge connecting Chincoteague and Assateague Islands, the main recommendation was widening it to allow emergency vehicles, as well as transit vehicles, to bypass any queued traffic. Participants also noted the need for shelters at the beach for bicyclists, pedestrians, and future transit riders.

7. Access for the Mobility-Impaired

Participants made many suggestions for improving access for the mobility-impaired, including beach wheelchairs, wheelchair matting for designated parking spaces, handicapped parking close to fishing sites, and a removable ramp for closer access to water and beach.

8. Marine Access

Some participants recommended providing ferries from the Wallops Island Visitor Center or sites on Chincoteague as well as improved private boat access, motorized and non-motorized, to Assateague Island.

9. Other

Other comments made by participants included suggestions for noise level standards and enforcement, changes in over-sand/off-road vehicle policy, improved access to various areas within CNWR and ASIS by all modes, including boat, and promotion or provision of alternative modes, including wagons pulled by ponies, a gondola or a ski lift. Providing beach-equipment concessions at Toms Cove was also recommended, to encourage visitors to use bicycles or a future transit service.

Notes from public outreach events appear in Appendix D.

Previous Surveys

Information on the transportation behavior and preferences of visitors was collected previously by surveys for three different studies. The first two studies only considered the Virginia district of ASIS while the 2007 Visitor Survey considered ASIS as a whole:

Chincoteague Visitor Transportation Needs Assessment Survey (1998)

This survey was funded by the Virginia Department of Transportation (VDOT) and conducted by Marketing Source, Inc. It was conducted August 20-23, and collected 310 intercept surveys in the Town of Chincoteague and 224 randomly distributed surveys from the entrance toll booths to CNWR and ASIS. Its intent was to "to assess transportation impacts, travel patterns, and mobility needs of visitors to Chincoteague and Assateague Islands during the peak tourist season."

The survey results indicated that most visitors use their car to travel to attractions and "about a third of visitors categorize traffic congestion and weekend parking on Main St., Maddox Rd. and at the Beach as a problem." Interest and support for transit and bicycle options was expressed in the survey results.

A large percentage of respondents in 1998 reported that they expected to use their car multiple times during the visit to travel to destinations on Chincoteague and Assateague. 26 percent of day visitors expected to use their cars 6 or more times or 11 or more times daily. It was unclear from the data whether people were reporting round-trip or one-way use.

About 60 percent of respondents stated that they were either very likely or somewhat likely to use trolley service with a 15-minute headway. Those who responded positively were more likely to be repeat tourists (one to three times in five years), visitors with young children, and first-time visitors, as opposed to frequent visitors (more than four times in five years) and visitors over 50 years old. Frequent visitors were more likely to rate weekend traffic and parking a problem. Most visitors supported the addition and improvement of bike trails, lanes, and racks adjacent to major thoroughfares.

Chincoteague Comprehensive Plan (2006)

This survey was conducted by the Town's consultants, Redman Johnston Associates, Ltd., to gauge public reaction to the Plan's recommendations and provide guidance to the planning process. 127 people completed the survey, with year-round residents (71 percent), seasonal (8 percent) and part-time (13 percent) residents represented. The transportation-related statements and responses were:

- Parking in the Downtown Area is adequate. No consensus. Almost half of respondents felt that parking in the Downtown Area is inadequate, although most respondents felt that parking was adequate most of the year except major summer holidays and Pony Penning Days. There was much uncertainty about the future adequacy of parking due to new development and the new Route 175 bridge. There was interest in providing additional, and more accessible, parking for older residents, visitors, and customers. Several respondents requested that no more parking lots be added in the Town of Chincoteague, with suggestions to instead focus on transit (in particular, for residents versus tourists), mainland parking, traffic circulation, and improved pedestrian and bicycle facilities.
- Pedestrian and bicycle facilities on Maddox Boulevard should be improved. Strong agreement. Over 80 percent of respondents agreed that pedestrian and bicycle facilities on Maddox Boulevard need improvement, including the addition of sidewalks and crosswalks along its entire length and designated lanes for bicycles (versus sidewalk use). Respondents did raise a concern that Maddox Boulevard was too narrow for many improvements, especially without eliminating on-street parking, which many regarded as important to keep. They also made it clear that widening was not feasible and/or not desirable. One suggestion was to reroute bicycles

elsewhere. Respondents also expressed concerns about the changes to traffic patterns and circulation resulting from the new bridge.

- <u>The Town should increase the number of pedestrian trails and bikeways throughout the community</u>. Strong agreement. 90 percent of respondents agreed that pedestrian and bicycle trails are important to both visitors and residents and should be extended and improved. Some expressed concern about dangerous conditions for both pedestrians and bicyclists, due to the volume of traffic, narrowness of the roads, and sharing of space. Respondents specifically identified other streets, including Church Street, Eastside, and Ridge/Chicken City Road

The survey also noted several additional requests for transportation facilities, including:

- A separate lane for small electric cars
- A shuttle system that would serve as alternative transportation to the beach
- A sidewalk from the Maddox Boulevard circle to Deep Hole Road and a bicycle trail to Assateague
- Launching facilities for non-motorized boats (canoes, kayaks, and shallow-draught, lightweight sailboats such as Sunfish) at the park in front of Chincoteague High School, with additional parking available at the school during the summer.

Assateague Island National Seashore Visitor Survey (2007)

This survey was prepared by the Eppley Institute for Parks and Public Lands, Indiana University and distributed throughout the Virginia and Maryland districts of Assateague from July 30 to August 12, 2006. 1,016 responses were received. The intent of the survey was to ascertain the motivations, expectations, interests, and needs of ASIS visitors.

The 2007 Assateague Island National Seashore Visitor Survey shows that most of the problems cited by visitors had to do with traffic (back-ups, parking scarcity) and facilities (bathrooms and water), though bathrooms were considered the most important concern by visitors. When asked what visitors liked least about their experience, parking and traffic flow was the second most frequently listed item (71), after bugs (386) and before weather (69). Parking and traffic flow was also listed third most frequently under suggestions for future planning for the park.

5 Peer Comparison and Best Practices

Advances in the implementation of innovative alternative transportation solutions have resulted in reduced congestion and improved safety for travelers. To build on the successful experiences of these solutions in locations similar to the Town of Chincoteague, Assateague Island National Seashore (ASIS) and Chincoteague National Wildlife Refuge (CNWR), a peer comparison study was conducted. The purpose of the peer comparison was to collect data about transportation solutions at sites and recreational attractions that share some characteristics with these locations. While the Town, ASIS and CNWR experience their own unique challenges and opportunities, there are still several locations throughout the U.S. that can share valuable learning experiences and best practices. The information gathered through the peer comparison form part of the basis for the generation of potential transportation alternatives.

Criteria and framework for assessment

The peer comparison effort was geared toward selecting locations that had implemented effective alternative transportation solutions and documented their successes and lessons learned, including: shared use paths, transit in various modes, intelligent transportation system solutions, and parking management systems. Locations that have been successful developing partnerships and securing funding for alternative transportation proposals are also highlighted in the summary.

Identification and selection

Peer sites were selected based on matching the criteria described above to locations discussed at the 2008 TAG meeting and at the Alternative Transportation Study's public meetings in October 2008 and January 2009. Additional sites were discussed with CNWR staff and the study's co-applicants. Based on this feedback, the following sites were chosen for the comparison:

- Gulf Islands National Seashore – Florida
- Cape Hatteras National Seashore – North Carolina
- Ocracoke Island – North Carolina
- Cape Cod National Seashore – Cape Cod, Massachusetts
- North Padre Island National Seashore – Texas
- Folly Beach - South Carolina

In addition, the following sites were investigated for specific issues:

- Sanibel Island/Ding Darling National Wildlife Refuge for the bicycle trail system
- South Ponte Vedra Beach for beach restoration
- Okemo Ski Resort for town-resort coordination on transportation management solutions

Detailed summaries of the research conducted for each site are included in Appendix E.

Based on the research, it was determined that two of the sites did not have any transportation solutions relevant to CNWR – North Padre Island National Seashore in Texas and South Ponte Vedra Beach in Florida.

Best Practice Summary

The sites with issues and solutions useful for CNWR are described below and organized by site with best practices at each location highlighted in the following categories: emergency transportation solutions, parking management, shuttle services, regional transit services, intelligent transportation systems, habitat protection, non-motorized and alternative transportation modes and planning initiatives for future services including regional coordination.

Gulf Islands National Seashore/Fort Pickens - Florida

Santa Rosa Island in Gulf Islands National Seashore (GUIS) is a barrier island approximately 50 miles long, between one-quarter to one-half mile wide. Visitation to this park is concentrated at Fort Pickens, an area of 1,700 acres located among the westernmost seven miles of Santa Rosa Island, near Pensacola Beach. During its peak operations, Fort Pickins attracted over 700,000 visitors per year. However, the damage sustained by the Fort Pickens Road from a series of weather related events severely limited access into the park which drastically reduced visitation. Understanding how GUIS worked to maintain access for visitors despite the loss of its main access road and plan for future alternative transportation solutions is the focus of the peer comparison.

1. Emergency Transportation Solutions

During the time of the road closure, additional services were implemented for visitors including an all-terrain vehicle shuttle service and ferry service using existing marine transportation operators. The reconstructed roadway opened on May 22, 2009. Construction of the roadway was funded by emergency funds due to hurricane damage and built by the Florida Department of Transportation. At the opening of the roadway, it was turned over to the National Park Service.

To provide information on park limitations due to lingering damage from the hurricanes, NPS created a flyer for summer 2009 for Fort Pickens including a map of the park and information on park hours, rules, and camping instructions. The flyer provides an important communication tool to keep visitors informed on current conditions in the park.

2. Regional Coordination Planning

Losing the only vehicular access road to the park heightened awareness of the park's vulnerability to storm activity and encouraged partners to further pursue initiating a ferry service to Fort Pickens. There has been a high level of interest for over 30 years to establish such a ferry service and the partners have been focused on being prepared when a funding opportunity arises. Planning for a future ferry service is a good example of the park and the City of Pensacola working collaboratively towards a future solution.

3. Regional Transit

The *Fort Pickens/Gateway Community Alternative Transportation Study* was completed in February 2009. The study explored expansion of current transit and trolley routes, and contingency plans for short and long-term road closures and discussed the potential extension of transit service into the park. Currently, a free seasonal beach trolley on Santa Rosa Island operated by the Santa Rosa Island Authority travels along Fort Pickens Road between the eastern edge of the Central Business District and Fort Pickens Gate, the park entrance. This service caters primarily to visitors in need of transportation for dining and evening entertainment. Although there is interest in expanding the service into Fort Pickens, it is unlikely in the near future since the current service is facing cutbacks due to financial pressures.

Figure 42. Santa Rosa Island Authority Beach Trolley Service

Source: http://www.visitpensacolabeach.com/find/ecat.asp

Cape Hatteras National Seashore – North Carolina

Cape Hatteras National Seashore is part of the Outer Banks, a series of barrier islands that stretch almost the entire length of the North Carolina coast. Cape Hatteras consists of approximately 72 miles of coastline encompassing over 24,000 acres, and varying in width from between one and three miles. Cape Hatteras is an interesting peer for this study due to its progress in implementing intelligent transportation systems to monitor traffic and flooding and inform travelers of travel conditions and emergencies. Habitat protection is also an issue that Cape Hatteras shares with CNWR.

1. Intelligent Transportation Systems

North Carolina Department of Transportation (NCDOT) plays an active role in monitoring travel conditions and flooding on roadways throughout Cape Hatteras in an effort to inform visitors of travel conditions and emergencies. A webcam and a variable message sign (VMS) are located at the Whalebone Junction park entrance. This location is a natural control point and the sign provides travelers important information regarding the condition of the ferry to Ocracoke and roads (including closures).   Standard messages on the VMS include information on road conditions including over wash, traffic crashes, and ferry shutdowns due to weather.

Additional cameras are installed and maintained by NCDOT on major roadways. TrafficLand, a for-profit company, hosts the traffic camera video and provides it at no charge to public agencies like NCDOT for their use in communicating real-time information on the web for both internal and public use.   For non-traffic information, Highway Advisory Radio is used on Cape Hatteras to communicate to the public, e.g. current advisories.

2. Habitat Protection

The NPS coordinates with the local municipalities regarding restrictions with off-road vehicle (ORV) access and closing areas due to shorebird and turtle nesting. These restrictions are to the result of a lawsuit by the Defenders of Wildlife and the National Audubon Society against the NPS. To communicate updates on restricted access, a link is provided on the NPS website to Google Earth, which provides a Beach Access Report issued every Thursday and is updated up to five times weekly during breeding season. The link states: "Once you have downloaded Google Earth, you can click on this beach access map link and zoom-in to the shoreline area in which you are interested to see the current access status."

Ocracoke Island – North Carolina

Ocracoke Island is part of the Cape Hatteras National Seashore. The entire island is owned by the National Park Service, except for the village. Access to the island is by ferry only – three routes operate: Hatteras (free), Swan Quarter (toll) and Cedar Island (toll). Ocracoke experiences some of the same issues as Chincoteague, including traffic congestion during peak visitation and vehicle conflicts with bicycles and pedestrians due to a lack of off-road facilities.

1. Non-Motorized Transportation

Congestion during peak times can be a safety issue since pedestrians, cyclists and vehicles must share the road. There are no sidewalks in the Village. Ocracoke and NCDOT are working in partnership to improve biking and walking on the island. NCDOT is seeking funding to improve on-road bicycle facilities from the NPS Pony Pens to the NPS campgrounds by widening the road three to four feet to accommodate bicyclists. The construction of the multi-use trail from the NPS' Campground to the NPS/Village of Ocracoke boundary has already been funded and construction is planned for fall 2009. The next phase for the trail from the camp grounds to the pony pen (seven miles) will be more difficult to move forward on due to environmental concerns.

Cape Cod National Seashore – Cape Cod, Massachusetts

Cape Cod National Seashore is located on 40 miles of shoreline on Cape Cod, a peninsula in Massachusetts cut off from the rest of the state by a man-made canal. Cape Cod acts as a barrier island shielding much of the Massachusetts coastline from Atlantic storms. The Seashore was established in 1961 to protect the natural, cultural, and recreational resources of over 43,500 acres in the Outer Cape, including land in six incorporated towns. In addition, the Seashore manages six beaches. The Seashore is accessible from the mainland only by one road, U.S. Highway 6, and otherwise by ferry via Provincetown, at its northern end. Over the past decade, the Cape Cod National Seashore has averaged between four and five million visits annually, with 60 percent of those visits coming during the peak season of June through September and mostly on weekends.

The Seashore and its adjacent communities face a number of transportation challenges, namely limited access, seasonal congestion, parking shortages, and erosion of parking areas. However, through partnerships, the Outer Cape has been able to implement a number of transit and non-motorized access solutions and is actively planning for improvements including: transit, bicycle access, and intelligent transportation systems (ITS) to aid in visitor information and emergency management.

1. Parking Management and Shuttle Services

In 1978, Coast Guard Beach experienced a significant erosion event when its parking area was destroyed in a powerful storm. A new parking lot inland was constructed at Little Creek with a free, seasonal park-operated shuttle providing access to the beach. Shuttle vehicles have a total capacity of 48 and consist of a gas-powered "power car" and trailer, both low-floor vehicles with an open configuration to accommodate beach gear. Capital funding for the shuttle is provided through the Federal Lands Highway Program, while operations funding is supplied by both admissions fees and the general park operating budget.

The issue of emergency evacuation at Coast Guard Beach is a concern for the Seashore since it does not have the capability to evacuate all the people who are on the beach at peak times. The weather is closely monitored and staff is alerted when a storm is approaching. The Seashore runs the shuttles as quickly as possible and directs people to the nearby shelter, a historical structure which currently houses the Cape Cod National Seashore overnight NEED (National Environmental Educational Development) program for school groups. Since the building can only accommodate a small fraction of visitors on the beach, the Seashore tries to warn visitors that they are at their own risk during storm events.

Figure 43. Coast Guard Beach Tram Vehicle

Source: Volpe Center photograph, October 2009.

2. *Regional Transit*

In addition to the Coast Guard Beach shuttle described above, the local regional transit authority operates two services nearby. In 2006, the Cape Cod Regional Transit Authority (CCRTA) began operating the Flex bus system on the Lower/Outer Cape, in partnership with the Cape Cod Commission, the regional planning agency, and the Seashore, which provided capital funding. Consisting of a fixed route integrated with a flexible, by-request concept, the Flex bus adheres to a set route and schedule, but is able to deviate from the established route by three-quarters of a mile by rider request. The ridership during the summer season is significantly higher than the rest of the year. The Flex buses are equipped with GPS and their real-time location can be viewed online. Operations funding comes from a town assessment based on the number of boardings per town.

Figure 44. Cape Cod Regional Transit Authority Flex.

Source: Volpe Center photograph, 2006.

The CCRTA also operates the Provincetown Shuttle, a seasonal bus line running from North Truro to Provincetown that serves both the Herring Cove Beach and the Province Lands Visitor Center, near Race Point Beach. It operates during the summer and fall months (May through October). The route is served by a traditional transit bus.

CCRTA is responsible for several other fixed routes throughout the rest of Barnstable County as well as an on-demand, paratransit service known as the "B-Bus."

3. Intelligent Transportation Systems

The National Seashore owns a variable message sign that provides real-time information on parking occupancy at Coast Guard, Nauset Light, and Marconi beaches. However, local residents and businesses have expressed concern about its appearance and impact on business, so its future use is uncertain.

Currently, the National Seashore is actively planning for ITS improvements to aid in visitor information and emergency management.

Folly Beach - South Carolina

Folly Beach is a barrier island, six miles long and the closest beach to Charleston, South Carolina. As of 2009, the City of Folly Beach's population is 2,333 people. Regional population including Charleston and North Charleston is 126,567. There are some similarities with Chincoteague/CNWR including: one main thoroughfare through the city (Center Street), issues with pedestrian and bicycle safety, and traffic congestion during peak visitation. However, there are also some differences – the city is located adjacent to the beach and most parking is free and on the street. There is only one hotel in Folly Beach; most visitors rent seasonal cottages.

1. Regional Transit

Public transportation to Folly Beach was recently initiated for travel from Charleston. The Charleston Area Regional Transportation Authority (CARTA) completed a two-month trial service in April and May 2009. Due to its success, the CARTA service resumed in late August on Saturdays and Sundays through October 18, to facilitate travel to the beach for students and other residents during the early fall months. It is likely that the service will continue as a six month seasonal route next spring through fall.

2. Non-Motorized Transportation

In an effort to improve non-motorized transportation options in Folly Beach, the Berkeley-Charleston-Dorchester Council of Governments (BCDCOG) recently contracted with a consultant for a transportation planning study. Discussions with BCDCOG's consultant indicated that the recommendations in the study will focus on improving pedestrian travel and reducing traffic congestion with the following interventions:

- Reduce Center Street from a four-lane roadway (two lanes in each direction) to one lane in each direction with a center median, angled parking and wider sidewalks.

- Limit access to side streets by gating them off during seasonal weekend peaks.

3. Alternative Transportation Modes

To reduce vehicle use for short trips, golf carts are allowed on all public roadways in Folly Beach with the exception of Center Street. A City ordinance describes the conditions of their use including the requirements for drivers. Information regarding the ordinance is available on the City's website and is provided at locations where golf carts are rented. The City website indicates the following: "City of Folly Beach Ordinances Enforced with Fines not to exceed $500.00."

Sanibel Island/Ding Darling National Wildlife Refuge – Sanibel, Florida

Sanibel Island is a barrier island located on the Gulf Coast of Florida near the City of Fort Myers. World famous for its migratory bird population, the J. N. "Ding" Darling National Wildlife Refuge is located on the island and has been identified as one of the largest undeveloped mangrove ecosystems in the United States. Encouraging biking and walking and reducing automobile use contributes to maintaining the sanctuary. The bicycle trail system developed by the City over thirty years ago as well as traffic management strategies for peak seasonal traffic is the focus of the peer comparison with Chincoteague.

1. Non-Motorized Transportation

Sanibel Island generally consists of two lane roads with an extensive shared-use path system used by bicycles and pedestrians. There is no outdoor lighting on the island including no traffic signals. Shared use paths are located all over the island and were mostly constructed between 1975 and 1996. Local citizens championed the initial effort and the paths were funded by the capital improvement program.

Since 2003, the City has completed over $2 million worth of improvements to the paths financed through the capital program. Damage from Hurricane Charley in August 2004 was instrumental in promoting the improvements on the main roadway through the City. Private partnerships which included the Chamber of Commerce have worked to make improvements happen.

There is no parking on City streets, so the paths provide a way to travel around the island. The City Manager worked with the MIS Department of the City to create an on-line interactive planning tool for the shared use paths - http://www.sanibeltrails.com/default.aspx.

Figure 45. Road and Bike Path, Sanibel.

Source: Volpe Center, photograph, August 2009.

The City has also worked to improve pedestrian safety. The death of an elderly pedestrian led the City to install mid-block pedestrian crosswalks with pedestrian crossing signage. These crossings provide a higher sense of awareness for drivers; they generally stop for bicyclists and pedestrians waiting to cross at the crosswalks. No pedestrian fatalities have occurred since their installation.

2. Traffic Management

The City has implemented a number of strategies to manage traffic congestion which are listed below:

- Traffic congestion on the island typically occurs between 2 and 6pm. During that time, police officers direct traffic at the intersections of Periwinkle Way/Causeway Road and Periwinkle Way/Casa Ybel Road.

- In the past, a variable message sign was posted before the Sanibel Causeway tolls to inform visitors if parking at the beaches was full. The sign was eliminated because of objections from the merchants on the island.

- Speed trailers are located on Causeway Road just past the bridge for traffic calming.

- In emergency situations, the City implements the following systems to notify residents and visitors: AM radio alerts, City website updates, automatic calling through 911 and reaching out to the local media.

Okemo Mountain Resort – Ludlow, Vermont

Okemo Mountain Resort is located in southern Vermont in the Village of Ludlow southeast of Rutland and northeast of Brattleboro. As a large New England ski resort, it attracts visitors from the larger metropolitan areas of New England and New York as well as local and regional day-trippers. Okemo offers an interesting peer comparison because of its effective working relationship with Ludlow and other nearby towns to address transportation issues which occur during peak ski season particularly on the rural roads leading to the resort and in the downtown commercial areas. Limited parking at the resort is also an issue.

1. Parking Management and Shuttle Services

A number of free shuttle services are provided by Okemo Mountain Resort to reduce traffic and parking congestion during peak periods. These services are paid for by Okemo as conditions of their permits with both the State of Vermont and the Town of Ludlow. The shuttles service the resort and the towns of Ludlow and Proctorsville. Okemo also supports a regional service provider (Connecticut River Transit) which services a number of nearby towns (Bellows Falls, Springfield and Chester).

At the mountain, Okemo has a main parking area with shuttles transporting skiers from their vehicles to the slopes. Skiing is a gear heavy sport which can make traveling from the parking area to the slopes difficult. The shuttles are equipped with side storage racks for skis and poles and overhead storage for bags and ski ambassadors (volunteers) assist skiers with their gear both on and off the vehicle. At the lodge, there are coin-operated lockers and Basket Room Storage (fee charged) in the base areas to store personal items. The Basket Room also offers overnight and multi-day storage options for personal belongings.

2. Traffic Management

Existing mitigation efforts to address traffic congestion include deploying traffic control officers at key locations at peak travel times. A traffic management plan is put into place when the number of vehicles parked at the main parking lots exceeds 1,100. The plan includes notifying the Towns of Ludlow and Chester and the Windsor County Sheriff. Traffic details are then placed at key locations to override the traffic signals.

Okemo has also employed strategies to encourage skiers to arrive and depart at off-peak times. To stagger arrivals at the mountain, the first hour of lift operations are free to let skiers try out the conditions before they purchase a lift ticket. Okemo also offers the "Sunday Solution Morning Half-Day Lift Ticket" which is valid from 8 a.m. to 1:30 p.m. for Vermont and New Hampshire residents only. It allows local skiers to head home early, therefore missing the peak traffic, without paying for a full-day lift ticket.

Solutions for CNWR

Based on the summaries of transportation solutions at peer sites, there are a number of feasible options and opportunities for CNWR to consider. These solutions are factored into the development of the interventions and alternatives described later in the report. These options include:

- Parking management and shuttle services for beach visitors (Cape Cod, Okemo)
- Regional transportation services (Cape Cod, Folly Beach, Okemo)
- Improvements to the bicycle/pedestrian network (Ocracoke, Sanibel Island, Folly Beach)

- Coordination with state, regional and local partners (Cape Cod, Okemo, Cape Hatteras, Ocracoke, Sanibel, Gulf Islands)

- Intelligent Transportation Systems (Cape Hatteras)

- Emergency Transportation Solutions (Gulf Island/Fort Pickens)

An important lesson indicated by the research for a number of the sites was the value of planning for future funding opportunities. Although it may be difficult to implement solutions with the current financial challenges facing both private and public agencies, preparing for future changes and developing partnerships can result in project implementation when funding becomes available.

A more detailed peer comparison report appears in Appendix E.

6 Transportation Alternatives

The existing conditions, public outreach, and peer comparison work presented in the foregoing chapters are the basis for the development and evaluation of transportation alternatives. The alternatives include "No Action" and three "action" scenarios, each of the latter comprising a group of transportation solutions. The partnership assessment began with the identification and characterization of candidate partners in the early stages of the project and then proceeded in tandem with the development of the alternatives. The results of the partnership assessment appear in Chapter 8.

Transportation alternatives framework: CNWR parking management

The candidate "action" alternatives correspond to the anticipated range of action alternatives now under development in the CCP, as understood from discussions with CNWR staff. The CCP consideration of the transportation system will focus on the options for managing and/or reconfiguring CNWR's public beach parking lots, which are:

- Retaining the lots as currently configured;
- Relocating the lots and/or reducing their capacity, or
- Eliminating the lots entirely.

The CCP alternatives represent escalating scope and effort. Each transportation "action" alternative is designed as an integrated group of solutions appropriate for the corresponding CCP alternative; the transportation alternatives are also of escalating scope and effort by CNWR and by its co-applicants and other partners. The alternatives also build upon each other such that each alternative includes the solutions set forth in the previous alternative (for example, Alternative 3 includes all of the solutions from Alternative 2). There are exceptions noted, as when a new or revised solution replaces a previous one or when a particular solution does not fit the new scenario.

Approach

The development of the transportation alternatives consisted of the following steps:

1. Identification of all possible "solutions", defined as individual actions or projects, either mode-specific items, technology improvements, or process enhancements (e.g., communications or partnerships)
2. Screening of solutions through review by CNWR and elimination of non-relevant and infeasible ones
3. Development of transportation alternative scenarios, including "No Action" and multiple "Action" alternatives
4. Assignment of the transportation solutions to the alternatives, to appropriately reflect the scenarios and to aim for sensible, integrated transportation systems
5. Characterization of the solutions and alternatives, that is, the implementation, time frame, cost, and political aspects of each

This process is followed by the development of evaluation criteria for the alternatives and the assessment of the alternatives (Chapter 7).

Transportation solutions

The Volpe Center developed a suite of transportation solutions based on problems and solutions identified by:

- Report of the Chincoteague Transportation Assistance Group (TAG), from meeting at CNWR in January 2008

- Project staff review of relevant transportation literature and related data

- Site visits and interviews with CNWR staff, co-applicants and other stakeholders

- Peer comparison (Chapter 5) showing transportation solutions to similar problems in other places

- Information provided by stakeholders during public meetings and other outreach measures as previously described (Chapter 4)

Each solution was intended to address one or more of the following desired outcomes:

- Reduce traffic congestion and improve traffic flow (generally from the mainland to the CNWR entrance, but specifically near the CNWR causeway and entrance);

- Alleviate parking pressure and provide parking options for CNWR visitors and seasonal travelers;

- Plan for long-term impact of coastal processes and climate change on location of, access to, and maintenance of, existing beach parking lots;

- Increase awareness of and access to educational and recreational resources other than the beach;

- Preserve access to natural resources while protecting those same natural resources;

- Provide as many options for access as possible as different users have different needs and preferences – this means consideration and accommodation of all modes, including individual vehicular access;

- Improve safe bicycle and pedestrian access;

- Improve emergency access and evacuation routes;

- Incorporate marine access, as appropriate; and

- Leverage partnerships and existing relationships among transportation stakeholders.

These outcomes also strongly reflect the goals of several related planning documents identified in Chapter 3, notably the Town of Chincoteague Comprehensive Plan and the Town of Chincoteague 2020 Transportation Plan.

The transportation solutions were placed in the following categories:

- Engineering/infrastructure. Engineering/infrastructure comprises construction and improvements of fixed transportation infrastructure (not including bicycle and pedestrian features), including solutions such as roadway widening, lane additions and reconfigurations, restriping, signage, and emergency shelters.

- Traffic management. Traffic management comprises operations, traveler information, and minor infrastructure solutions, including signalization changes, signage and way-finding interventions, and intelligent transportation systems (ITS) features.

- Parking and parking management. Parking and parking management includes solutions for private vehicle parking, including transit links, satellite parking and new structures, parking area amenities, and information for travelers.

- Bicycles and pedestrian improvements. Bicycle and pedestrian improvements comprise hard infrastructure (e.g., sidewalks and multi-use paths and trails), incorporation of bicycle and transit access, and information enhancements.

- Transit. Transit includes new and reconfigured routes and services, and transit vehicles including conventional and small transit vehicles, alternative fuel vehicles, vans, and trolleys.

Solutions considered but not pursued

The project team and CNWR decided not to pursue several of the initially identified possible solutions, because they would be infeasible, redundant, or inappropriate in the context of this study. These appear as underlined text in the following bullets, each accompanied by a brief explanation for its elimination.

- **Engineering/infrastructure**

  o Beach and beach parking protection strategies (dunes, sand replenishment, jetties, snow fencing). This group of solutions was removed from consideration in this study after discussion and agreement with CNWR, because they are properly within the scope of the Refuge's CCP and Seashore's GMP processes and such activity would be contrary to the NPS Management Policies (2006), which states that NPS will "Natural shoreline processes (such as erosion, deposition, dune formation, overwash, inlet formation, and shoreline migration) will be allowed to continue without interference" (Section 4.8.1.1).

- **Traffic Management**

  o Structure daily fees so that it is more expensive to purchase and enter during peak hours to distribute visitation. Implementation would be difficult in the context of the current fee structure and in the future if proposed off-site purchase are put into effect.

  o Implement automated pass-reader system (e.g., "E-Z Pass"). This system would be one of several operational features at a new, dedicated fee booth and would require construction of an extra traffic lane, whose intent would be to ease congestion at the Beach Road entry point. This booth would also serve for collection of pre-paid passes, expedited passage of vehicles displaying long term passes, and access for transit vehicles.

    There are many uncertainties about the hardware, software, operation, and maintenance of an automated system, and the benefits of the extra fee booth would be largely realized through other features that expedite fee purchase and collection.

  o Partner with NASA and Coast Guard to develop a joint evacuation plan of federal lands in the area. There is currently an evacuation plan that covers the study area, and federal managers review and update it on a regular basis.

  o Evaluate traffic calming strategies to address speeding and modal conflicts in the Town and in CNWR, with speed humps, roundabouts, landscaped medians, and signage. Data review and discussion with CNWR and the Town indicate that speeding is not a serious issue. However, this item could be evaluated in a future corridor planning study, with a focus on Maddox Boulevard.

- **Parking Management**

  o During peak visitation, use the Wildlife Loop for additional parking. This new use of the Wildlife Loop would not align with the Refuge's mission and goals; for example, it would compete with other uses of Wildlife Loop, for wildlife observation and recreation.

  o Develop new bayside beach and parking lot, accessible by Beach Road. The idea included the assumption that the landward natural movement of the island will create more sand on the bayside and allow for a new beach destination that would provide safer, shallow waters for children to play and swim in. Site visits revealed a lack of sufficient land to add parking on the Toms Cove side and the near proximity of the existing beach lots means that they would likely serve the "new" beach when and if it comes into being.

- o Develop existing pony corral area into new parking area and access point to beach and bay. This proposal is not currently being considered because it would require significant environmental study and mitigation of the existing wetlands on the site and would require the pony corrals to be relocated somewhere else.

- **Bicycle/pedestrian**

  - o None.

- **Transit**

  - o None.

- **Marine**

The marine transportation solutions considered focused on marine passenger transport as an alternative to automobiles and terrestrial transit. The management of small boat access to CNWR, including both powered and non-motorized craft, and its supporting infrastructure supports an important recreational and educational function, but does not represent a transportation mode that can significantly reduce automobile traffic into and around CNWR.

There is not a good opportunity for effective passenger vessel service directly to the public beach because of depth restrictions at the closest landing point in inner Toms Cove. A dock there would have to be at least 150 yards long and would represent a significant viewshed impact, especially from the ASIS Visitor Center, as well as causing other ecological impacts in the Toms Cove marsh. New infrastructure here would require an environmental impact assessment and, if undertaken, would probably entail high construction cost. Furthermore, the nor'easter of November 2009 demonstrated the volatile and changing nature of the land form and the navigating conditions in and around Toms Cove. Service and infrastructure investments would have uncertain long-term prospects in this dynamic environment.

The Assateague Lighthouse Landing would be suitable for modest passenger service, bringing visitors, especially small groups, to the Lighthouse and the FWS Visitor Center, and providing access to CNWR's bike trails. The existing infrastructure could be suitably improved at low cost. The East Side Drive boat ramp would be the most sensible departure point on Chincoteague Island, if a suitable ramp and floating dock could be provided there and if a shared use parking arrangement can be agreed upon with the Town.

The former U.S. Coast Guard Station should be viewed as a potential educational and historical destination in the long term, but would likely require significant planning, environmental compliance, and refurbishment of dock and other landing infrastructure. Access from the water would then suitable for a small passenger boat, and the most sensible mainland departure point would be Curtis Merritt Harbor. The beach erosion caused by the November 2009 nor'easter indicates a future where marine transportation may be the only means of access to the Station.

Summary. Marine passenger transport is not a good candidate for relieving congestion and parking capacity problems associated with high volume visitation days at the public beach. However, there is a short-term, relatively low expense opportunity to provide a modest boat service to the Lighthouse Landing, targeted to groups, and a long-term, high-expense opportunity to bring visitors to the former U.S. Coast Guard Station on Toms Cove Hook.

- **Other items**

    o <u>Wagons pulled by ponies</u>. This idea is probably best suited as an interpretive opportunity for visitors rather than a form of alternative transportation. Its capacity would be so limited as to have little effect in reducing demand for other transportation modes, and the wagons might themselves contribute to traffic congestion.

    o <u>Gondola</u>. Gondolas have been proposed in several non-alpine settings in recent years, but have not yet found acceptance as a people-moving asset. They are most likely infeasible for CNWR and the Town of Chincoteague due to very high capital and running costs, safety and security concerns, environmental impact, impact on viewscapes, and the operational and program commitments required of its owners.

    o <u>Noise level standards and enforcement</u>. This was determined to be outside the scope of this study and should be considered in the CNWR CCP and ASIS GMP processes; however, some of the identified solutions could help reduce noise levels by promoting non-motorized and alternative fuel use.

    o <u>Changes in over-sand/off-road vehicle policy</u>. Off-road vehicles are outside the scope of this study and will be addressed in the ASIS GMP and CNWR CCP.

Alternative 1 - No Action

The "No Action" alternative includes no transportation solutions; thus the characterization of Alternative 1 is a compendium of issues and concerns raised by CNWR and the co-applicants (Table 8).

Note that safety-related items appear in red font in all the tables describing the alternatives in this chapter, reflecting CNWR's and the co-applicants' high concern in that area.

Table 8. Alternative 1 – No Action.

Alternative 1 - No Action		
	Transportation Status Quo	**Concerns and Consequences**
Engineering/ Infrastructure	Lack of consistent pavement markings to indicate travel lanes, shoulders, and parking on Maddox Blvd and Main Street.	Safety concerns for VDOT and Town of Chincoteague. Less efficient multi-modal travel.
	No shelters on the beach for emergencies/storms	Safety concern for CNWR: exposure to severe weather, especially for visitors accessing the beach via transit and bike/ped. Barrier to people using transit and non-motorized modes.
	Beach Road Bridge lacks bypass capability to easily accommodate transit vehicles and emergency vehicle.	Safety concern for CNWR: emergency response delays during congested conditions. Limitation of transit opportunities due to delays.
	Route 175: Lack of shoulders and emergency pull-off areas (as recommended in VHB Route 13 Corridor Study) on Route 175. Lack of signage for Queens Sound turn. Lack of speed control interventions. Lack of real time traffic/emergency monitoring.	Unsafe road conditions. Emergency response difficulties. Poor access for bicycles/pedestrians.
	Lack of siren notification system at ASIS beach for emergency evacuation and/or storm warnings.	Safety concern for ASIS: lack of advanced severe weather warning and potential exposure of visitors.
	Limited handicapped accessibility at ASIS beach	Access concern for ASIS, leading to poor public perception and negative visitor experience.
Traffic Management	No off-site pass purchasing; no provision at fee booths for pre-purchases.	Lack of promotion for CNWR; inconvenience and booth delays for visitors.
	Limited traffic management measures, special event and peak weekend traffic routing using variable message signs.	Increased congestion in and around CNWR, leading to negative visitor experience and air quality impact.
	No pre-trip planning information on fees, peak beach visitation times (no website, 800 number)	In CNWR, exacerbates congestion and delays at fee booths during peak times.
	Poor real time traffic/parking information over existing CNWR AM radio, FM radio, and website	No notification system for full CNWR beach parking lots, resulting in traffic delays, visitor frustration, increased emissions, and congestion.
	CNWR emergency notification is on a case-by-case basis.	Response by CNWR staff is labor and time intensive. Coordination may be difficult.
	Available CNWR maps do not clearly show parking locations, shelters, handicapped facilities, and emergency evacuation procedures.	Delays at the CNWR fee booths and extra driving in CNWR, leading to more congestion and air pollution, and a poor visitor experience.
Parking and Parking Management	Existing unpaved beach parking lots.	Many visitors prefer using these lots. However, there is storm damage annually, at times serious (e.g., 2009 Ida Nor'easter). Long term shoreline changes may result in total loss of the parking lots. ASIS incurs annual O/M costs of $100-600K in years of normal storm activity and costs can be higher when major storms hit.
	No designated offsite beach parking .	No parking options during summer peak days or when beach lot capacity is reduced due to severe weather. Limits potential of transit into the Refuge.
Bicycles and Pedestrians	Gaps in bike trails and lanes, in particular between the Town of Chincoteague and CNWR.	Unsafe conditions. Barrier to bicycle use.
	Sidewalk gaps on main Town thoroughfares. Lack of crosswalks, pedestrian signals at signalized intersections.	Unsafe conditions. Barrier to pedestrian use.
	Poorly developed bicycle maps and signage, and limited distribution of educational outreach materials	Unsafe behavior. Barrier to bicycle use.
Transit	No transit service to CNWR.	No mitigation of beach traffic congestion. No alternative access to beach or other Refuge sites, in particular when beach lot capacity is reduced or when lots are full.
	Trolleys do not accommodate bicycles or other recreational gear.	Barrier to bicycle use; inhibits potential of transit to beach.
	Current transit routes overlap and are long and circuitous.	Discourages ridership.

Alternatives 2 through 4 characteristics

The CCP alternatives represent escalating scope and effort. Each transportation "action" alternative is an integrated group of solutions appropriate for the corresponding CPP alternative. Transportation alternatives 2 through 4 also represent escalating scope and effort by CNWR, its co-applicants, and other partners. Each alternative includes the solutions set forth in the previous alternative, with exceptions noted.

Each of the three "action" alternatives is presented as a brief summary accompanied by a table. The tables list solutions and show the "owners" (i.e., those entities that would be primarily responsible for the action) and partners for each solution, and describe implementation requirements, the estimated time frame to implement, the potential political difficulties, and the cost. There are ratings of the relative scope or difficulty involved: "High", "Medium", and "Low". The rating terms are defined in Table 9. Note that for the cost characterization only the terms "Very High" and "Very Low" are included, to better address the wide range of costs for the contemplated solutions. Volpe Center project staff considered each solution and assigned the ratings collaboratively, followed by a review by CNWR and the co-applicants.

The entities appearing most commonly as owners and partners in the tables are abbreviated or shortened as follows:

Assateague Island National Seahore	ASIS
Chincoteague National Wildlife Refuge	CNWR
Town of Chincoteague	Town
Accomack County	County
Virginia DOT	VDOT
Chamber of Commerce	Chamber

There are more detailed characterizations of the alternatives and solutions in a corresponding series of tables in Appendix F. The actual capital cost estimates appear in these tables; details as to the cost calculations and methods also appear in Appendix F.

Table 9. Alternatives Descriptions and Ratings.

RATING	DESCRIPTION			
	Implementation	Time Frame	Political	Cost
VERY HIGH				Same as "high" cost, except capital cost exceeds $100,000.
HIGH	Multiple stages, which may include planning, design, environmental compliance (e.g., NEPA, state laws, public hearings/comments/etc.), other permitting requirements (e.g., Town board approvals, zoning reviews, etc.) and cooperative agreements, and will usually include acquisition or construction of significant new capital assets, and significant maintenance and operation requirements afterward.	4 or more years to implement	High visibility, high impact item likely to attract publicity and controversy, particularly from local commercial interests and Town and County government officials. Public processes raise profile.	Required new infrastructure/equipment/etc. necessitates new budget request $25,000 - $100,000. Added O/M and other running costs will be sufficient to revise annual projections for labor, spare parts, consumables, and/or other items. Cost estimates prepared for capital items and, to the extent practicable, for added running costs.
MEDIUM	Planning that may include minimal design, small scale cooperative agreements, acquisition of small capital assets; will not include construction of infrastructure or significant environmental compliance work (e.g., NEPA, state law, public hearings). May include operational requirements and minimal maintenance needs.	2-3 years to implement	Scale or nature of solution make it less likely to attract significant publicity, and minor or non-existent public processes keep profile low. Some particular interest groups may have objections, but it is likely that most users and residents will be favorably disposed.	Required new infrastructure/equipment/etc. necessitates new budget request, i.e., in the range $5,000 - $25,000. Added O/M and other running costs will be sufficient to revise annual projections for labor, spare parts, consumables, and/or other items. Cost estimates prepared for capital items and, to the extent practicable, for added running costs.
LOW	Minimal or no planning functions; low or non-existent new capital assets; low effort operations and/or maintenance.	1 year or less to implement	No public reviews or public input process; low visibility and low impact imply non-controversial or likely to have very small percentage of people opposed. Or, the value and benefit of more significant projects ("high" or "medium" implementation) are likely to be viewed favorably by a very high majority of users and residents.	Minimal start-up/acquisition costs (< $5,000) may be required, but can likely be covered with available money in the owner's budget, and that added O/M costs will be minor. Cost estimates will not be prepared for these items .
VERY LOW				Existing infrastructure/ equipment/etc., if needed at all, are sufficient AND that there will be no added O/M or other running costs.

Alternative 2: Maintain existing beach parking

In this alternative, ASIS and CNWR would maintain the beach parking lots in their current configuration and capacity, thus continuing to incur the associated annual operations and maintenance costs. The parking capacity at the beach would continue to be exceeded ten to twenty days per year. The transportation solutions mainly address traffic congestion, safety (especially for bicyclists and pedestrians), and improved traveler information, without significant infrastructure or operational solutions for parking. Most of these solutions represent quickly-implementable improvements to the status quo, require Low and Medium effort to implement, have short time frames, and are Low cost. Nearly all of these solutions are non-controversial and should require minimal outreach and political effort.

The primary safety-related solutions are four roadway infrastructure projects on the Route 175 Causeway and Maddox Boulevard. These justify quick action, but entail Medium effort, time, and expense (total capital expense estimated at $166,000). There is also a safety solution for within CNWR: siren notification system at the beach costing about $35,000. These solutions make sense under Alternatives 3 and 4 as well and are all assumed to be brought forward as part of those alternatives.

The Alternative 2 solutions and description ratings appear in Table 10. Map 21 is a map of the study area showing locations of the solutions.

Table 10. Alternative 2 Description.

	Transportation Solutions	Owner	Partners	Implement-ation	Time Frame	Political	Cost
Engineering/ Infrastructure	Provide consistent pavement markings to indicate travel lanes, shoulders, and parking on Maddox Blvd and Main Street.	VDOT	Town	MEDIUM	MEDIUM	LOW	MEDIUM
	On Route 175 Causeway, install signage to indicate turning vehicles at Queens Sound.	VDOT	County	LOW	MEDIUM	LOW	LOW
	Eliminate passing zones on the Route 175 Causeway.	VDOT	County	MEDIUM	MEDIUM	MEDIUM to HIGH	MEDIUM
	Install center lane and shoulder rumble strips along Route 175 Causeway.	VDOT	County	MEDIUM	MEDIUM	LOW	MEDIUM
	Improve handicapped accessibility through several interventions such as: install ADA matting to designate handicapped parking in beach parking lots, re-introduce a removable beach ramp to provide improved access to wheelchair users.	CNWR/ASIS	None	LOW	MEDIUM	LOW	LOW

Table 10 continued, next page.

Table 10. Alternative 2 Description (continued).

	Transportation Solutions	Owner	Partners	Implement-ation	Time Frame	Political	Cost
Traffic Management	Provide off-site pass purchasing at public nodes (e.g., Chamber of Commerce, Virginia Welcome Center). Person-to-person transactions.	CNWR/ASIS	Town, Chamber, Virginia Welcome Center(s)	MEDIUM	MEDIUM	LOW	LOW
	Provide pre-trip planning information on fees, peak beach visitation times, and options for beach access (including handicapped) through website and an 800 number.	CWNR/ASIS	None	LOW	LOW	LOW	LOW
	Provide pre-trip planning information on fees, peak beach visitation times, and options for beach access (including handicapped) at kiosk at the Virginia Welcome Center.	CWNR/ASIS	VDOT	LOW	LOW	LOW	LOW
	Use existing CNWR AM radio frequency to deliver standard messages and updated traffic/parking information.	CWNR/ASIS	None	MEDIUM	LOW	LOW	MEDIUM
	Continue use of local FM radio station to deliver standard messages and updated traffic/parking information.	CWNR/ASIS	Radio Station WCTG 96.6 FM	LOW	LOW	LOW	VERY LOW
	Implement siren notification system in CNWR (including speakers at the beach) for emergency evacuation and/or storm warnings.	CWNR/ASIS	None	MEDIUM	MEDIUM	MEDIUM	MEDIUM
	Improve directional and informational signage at specific points on Chincoteague to supplement CNWR maps (e.g., Route 175 causeway/ Maddox Boulevard interesection, Chamber of Commerce rotary, Beach Road at CNWR rotary and after fee booths).	VDOT	CNWR/ASIS, Town	MEDIUM	MEDIUM	MEDIUM	MEDIUM
	Designate one booth for pre-purchased passes.	CWNR/ASIS	None	LOW	MEDIUM	LOW	VERY LOW
	Revise CNWR to clearly show all destinations, parking locations and shelters, and identify additional important notices including handicapped facilities, bicycling etiquette in the refuge and emergency evacuation procedures.	CNWR/ASIS	None	MEDIUM	MEDIUM	LOW	LOW
Parking and Parking Management	Provide designated area in existing beach parking lots for small motorized vehicles, including motorcycles, scooters and electric carts. Include storage lockers (could be used for bicyclists also).	CWNR/ASIS	Chamber, rental companies	LOW	MEDIUM	LOW	LOW
	Add parking lot information to CNWR map and other online and print materials.	CWNR/ASIS	None	LOW	MEDIUM	LOW	LOW
Bicycles and Pedestrians	Construct trail between the NPS bridge and the Chamber of Commerce traffic circle.	CNWR/ASIS	VDOT, Town	HIGH	Work starts 2010	LOW	HIGH
	Develop improved bicycle maps (including all CNWR routes and those identified in Town and VDOT planning documents), signage (e.g., "Share the road"), and educational outreach materials, to be distributed by lodging and other businesses in Chincoteague.	Town	CNWR/ASIS, bicycle rental companies	MEDIUM	MEDIUM	LOW	LOW
Transit	Shorten the existing green Pony Express Route to route that goes from Community Center to HS (via Hallie Wealton Drive), then along Main Street to Bunting, then up Ridge Road to Maddox, and to Oyster Museum and back via Deep Hole Road to the Community Center. Red route stays the same.	Pony Express	CNWR/ASIS, Town	MEDIUM	MEDIUM	LOW	LOW
	Extend the route above as a pilot for May and September (weekends and holidays only, 9am-5pm or so) to sites within the Refuge Wildlife Loop/Lighthouse, FWS VC, NPS VS/Beach. No new vehicles required.	Pony Express	CNWR/ASIS Town	MEDIUM	MEDIUM	LOW	MEDIUM
	Implement a commercial special use permit for beach equipment concessions at beach (umbrellas, chairs, etc.) to provide gear for visitors who access beach by bicycle or walking.	CNWR/ASIS	Concess-ioners or CUP entities	MEDIUM	MEDIUM	MEDIUM	LOW

Map 21. Alternative 2 Solutions.

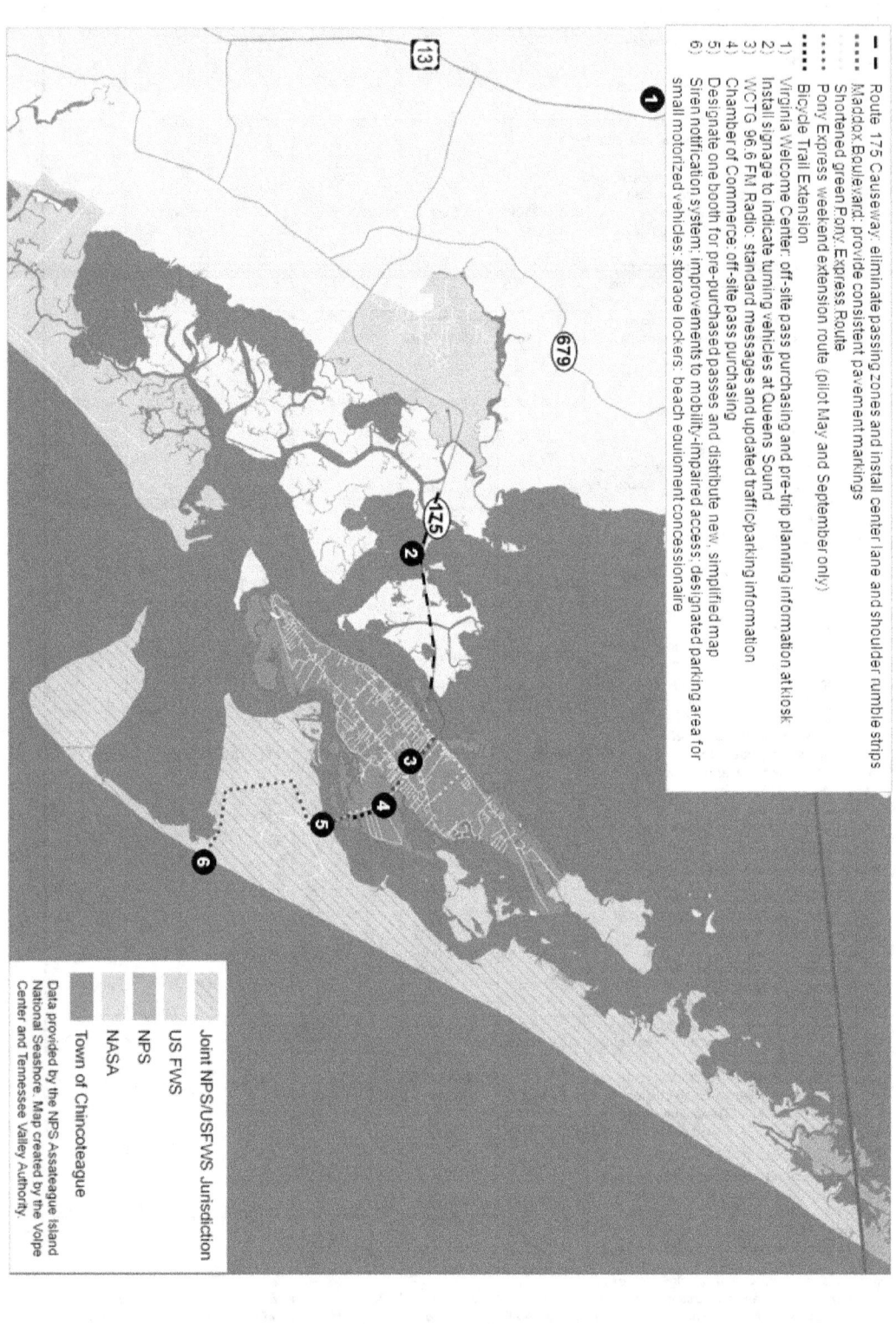

- – – Route 175 Causeway: eliminate passing zones and install center lane and shoulder rumble strips
- ••••• Maddox Boulevard: provide consistent pavement markings
- ••••• Shortened green Pony Express Route
- ••••• Pony Express weekend extension route (pilot May and September only)
- ••••• Bicycle Trail Extension
- 1) Virginia Welcome Center: off-site pass purchasing and pre-trip planning information at kiosk
- 2) Install signage to indicate turning vehicles at Queens Sound
- 3) WCTG 96.6 FM Radio: standard messages and updated traffic/parking information
- 4) Chamber of Commerce: off-site pass purchasing
- 5) Designate one booth for pre-purchased passes and distribute new, simplified map
- 6) Siren notification system: improvements to mobility-impaired access; designated parking area for small motorized vehicles; storage lockers; beach equipment concessionaire

Joint NPS/USFWS Jurisdiction
US FWS
NPS
NASA
Town of Chincoteague

Data provided by the NPS Assateague Island National Seashore. Map created by the Volpe Center and Tennessee Valley Authority.

Solutions not included on map: provide pre-trip planning information through website and an 800 number; use existing CNWR AM frequency to deliver standard messages and updated traffic/parking information; improve directional and informational signage; create simple map focused on access; develop improve bicycle maps and educational outreach materials.

Alternative 3: Relocate and/or reduce beach parking

In this alternative, the capacity of the beach parking lots would be reduced, either in their current location or relocated north to uplands behind the beach. This action is a major shift from the parking management approach that has been in place for many years, and would necessitate and facilitate many significant improvements in the transportation system. If the scenario were to include relocation of the lots north to the uplands, vehicular access would be rerouted, most likely via the Wildlife Loop. This project would be costly and involve a difficult environmental review process and significant public opposition. The CCP process would address the particulars of this action, if ASIS/CNWR choose to examine it.

This group of transportation solutions therefore entails higher effort to implement and has longer time frames, higher costs, and more political challenges. They address a new situation where, on busy summer days, many more visitors would park outside ASIS/CNWR and travel to the beach by alternate means. Moreover, the reduced size of the parking lots at the beach would probably result in many more days each year where beach parking capacity is exceeded. Alternative 3 represents strong, concerted actions to prevent exacerbation of congestion and the attendant problems of pollution, visitor frustration, and deterioration of roadway safety.

The safety-related solutions are High effort, time, and cost, particularly adding a bicycle/pedestrian footbridge and reconfiguring the Assateague Channel Bridge for a third vehicle lane (approximately $3.3M, including environmental compliance activities) and the provision of shoulders and emergency pullouts on the Route 175 Causeway ($5M). Sidewalk and crossing improvements in Chincoteague address safety and improved mobility and access and are Medium effort, time, and cost, but may be politically challenging because of perceived impacts on affected homes and businesses.

Alternative 3 envisions the first stage of a transportation system to move people from off-site parking facilities to the public beach, through traffic and parking management, transit improvements, and ITS and information solutions, including those identified in Alternative 2. The result of full implementation for the arriving visitor would be:

- Advance knowledge of transportation and parking options, and an option for advance purchase of the entrance fee;
- Real-time knowledge of the status of the beach parking lots and the opportunity to decide between parking off-site and visiting other attractions in Chincoteague;
- Easily accessible satellite parking (probable sites: Chincoteague High School, Chincoteague Elementary School, and the Chincoteague Community Center); and
- Convenient, reliable shuttle service between the satellite parking and the beach, with accommodations on the vehicles for beach gear, bicycles, and other sundries.

The eleven traffic and parking management solutions are all Medium to High implementation effort, time, and cost, and most of them have some potential element of controversy, either with local government and business interests or because of potential environmental impacts; the total estimated cost of these is $832,000 ($312,000 for solutions owned by CNWR/ASIS, not including $1.6M for the relocation of beach parking lots north of their current location). There is one operational transit solution to extend service to satellite parking and one to add bike racks; these are Low effort and cost items.

The bicycle and pedestrian solutions are Medium to High implementation effort, time, and cost make sense within the context of the major transportation shift implied in Alternative 3, as alternative transportation modes assume greater prominence. This includes the trail between the end of the Black Duck Trail and the beach, which would complete a safe bicycle and walking path within CNWR. The beach concessions identified in Alternative for bicyclists and pedestrians also appear here as an amenity available to transit riders.

All the transportation solutions of Alternative 2 would still be in place. Alternative 3 solutions and ratings appear in Table 11. Map 22 is a map of the study area showing locations of the solutions.

Table 11. Alternative 3.

	Transportation Solutions	Owner	Partners	Implement-ation	Time Frame	Political	Cost
Engineering/ Infrastructure	Construct shelters on the beach for emergencies/storms for visitors accessing the beach via transit and bike/ped.	CWNR/ASIS	None	HIGH	MEDIUM	MEDIUM	HIGH
	Reconfigure Assateague Channel Bridge for three vehicle lanes, for transit vehicles and emergency vehicle access, and build new ~12-foot wide bridge to provide bicycle/pedestrian access into CNWR; includes widening Beach Road between bridge and fee booths at current or re-located site.	CNWR/ASIS	None	HIGH	HIGH	HIGH	VERY HIGH
	Construct shoulders and additional emergency pull-off areas (as recommended in VHB Route 13 Corridor Study) on Route 175 Causeway.	VDOT	County, Town	HIGH	HIGH	MEDIUM	VERY HIGH
Traffic Management	Relocate fee booths east, further from the bridge, to provide additional storage capacity for queuing vehicles and to accommodate an express lane.	CNWR/ASIS	None	HIGH	MEDIUM	HIGH	HIGH
	Provide real-time information on parking availability at the beach and at off-site locations, through variable message signs at the foot of the Route 175 bridge into Chincoteague and the Chamber of Commerce traffic circle, using data obtained from vehicle detectors	CWNR/ASIS	Chamber, VDOT, Town	MEDIUM	MEDIUM	HIGH	HIGH
	Provide detailed information for visitors at hotels, campgrounds and the Chamber of Commerce on peak visitation times, options for beach access, and real-time information on beach parking/traffic conditions (likely via website).	CWNR/ASIS/ Town	Chamber, Town	MEDIUM	MEDIUM	LOW	LOW
	Install cameras to monitor traffic on the Route 175 causeway for improved incident management and variable message signs on Routes 175 (one) and 13 (two)	VDOT	County,Town, TrafficLand	MEDIUM	MEDIUM	LOW	HIGH
	Implement special event and peak weekend traffic routing using variable message signs and/or traffic signal timing in response to real-time traffic conditions.	VDOT	CNWR/ASIS, County, Town	LOW	MEDIUM	HIGH	LOW

Table 11 continued, next page.

Table 11. Alternative 3 (continued).

	Transportation Solutions	Owner	Partners	Implement-ation	Time Frame	Political	Cost
Parking and Parking Management	Construct new parking lot for beach north of current lots, of similar or reduced capacity, accessible by existing service road (requires environmental assessment). Site should be in a more protected area (limited severe weather impacts) with consideration for emergency access and shelter.	CWNR/ASIS	None	HIGH	HIGH	HIGH	VERY HIGH
	Provide drop-off area for gear and people at beach parking lots. Driver would then return to satellite parking lot and bicycle or take a shuttle back to the beach (also consider in design for new lot).	CWNR/ASIS	Shuttle service provider, Town	LOW	MEDIUM	LOW	LOW
	Reduce parking capacity at beach front lots.	CWNR/ASIS	None	HIGH	HIGH	HIGH	HIGH
	Close Assateague Island to personal vehicles during peak hours during peak season (July and August weekends, 10 am to 2 pm).	CWNR/ASIS	VDOT, County, Town	LOW	MEDIUM	HIGH	LOW
	Designate existing community and public parking lots for peak seasonal beach parking, to be serviced by shuttle. Parking lots could include the parking lots at the Chincoteague Center and Town Hall, the High School, and the Elementary School.	Town	CNWR/ASIS, Cty Schools, shuttle service provider	HIGH	MEDIUM	HIGH	LOW
	Implement ITS system to track real-time beach parking lot occupancy and feed into variable message signs.	CWNR/ASIS	VDOT, County, Town	LOW	MEDIUM	HIGH	LOW
Bicycles and Pedestrians	Construct trail between the end of the Black Duck Trail and the beach to provide safe bicycle and walking paths in CNWR.	CWNR/ASIS	None	MEDIUM	MEDIUM	MEDIUM	MEDIUM
	Sidewalk improvements and/or construction along both sides of Maddox Blvd. to fill in gaps from Beach Road bridge to Chicken City Road (provide prioritized list).	VDOT	Town	HIGH	MEDIUM	HIGH	VERY HIGH
	Install crosswalks, pedestrian pushbuttons, and signals for ped/bikes to safely cross at signalized intersections on Maddox and Main Streets, Chicken City Road, Deep Hole Road. Consider No Right Turn on Red restrictions and leading pedestrian signal timing (head start for crossing). High visibility crosswalks and signage at the Chamber of Commerce traffic circle.	VDOT	Town	HIGH	MEDIUM	MEDIUM	HIGH
Transit	Create permanent daytime service into CNWR from May through September, weekends and holidays only. This route will also serve any new satellite parking areas. No new vehicles required.	Pony Express or other service	CNWR/ASIS, Town	MEDIUM	MEDIUM	LOW	MEDIUM
	Modify existing Pony Express vehicles to add bicycle racks, and accommodation for other gear	Pony Express	CNWR/ASIS, Town	MEDIUM	MEDIUM	LOW	LOW
	Implement a commercial special use permit for beach equipment concessions at beach (umbrellas, chairs, etc.) to provide gear for visitors who access beach by transit	CNWR/ASIS	Concessioners or CUP entities	MEDIUM	MEDIUM	MEDIUM	LOW

Map 22. Alternative 3 Solutions.

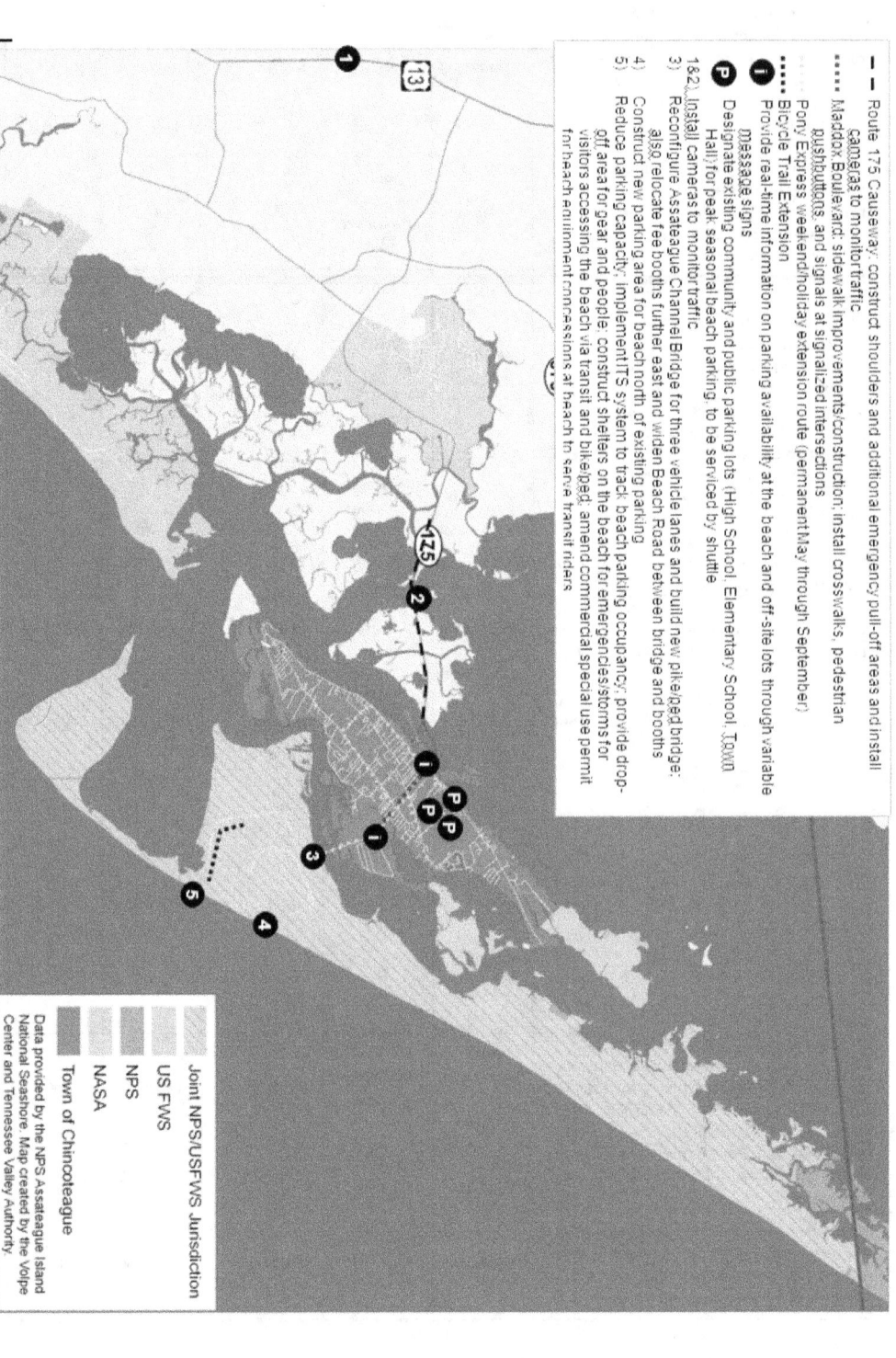

– – Route 175 Causeway: construct shoulders and additional emergency pull-off areas and install cameras to monitor traffic

••••• Maddox Boulevard: sidewalk improvements/construction; install crosswalks, pedestrian pushbuttons, and signals at signalized intersections

•••• Pony Express weekend/holiday extension route (permanent May through September)

•••• Bicycle Trail Extension

i Provide real-time information on parking availability at the beach and off-site lots through variable message signs

P Designate existing community and public parking lots (High School, Elementary School, Town Hall) for peak seasonal beach parking, to be serviced by shuttle

1&2. Install cameras to monitor traffic.

3) Reconfigure Assateague Channel Bridge for three vehicle lanes and build new pike/ped bridge; also relocate fee booths further east and widen Beach Road between bridge and booths

4) Construct new parking area for beach north of existing parking

5) Reduce parking capacity; implement ITS system to track beach parking occupancy; provide drop-off area for gear and people; construct shelters on the beach for emergencies/storms for visitors accessing the beach via transit and bike/ped; amend commercial/special use permit for beach equipment concessions at beach to serve transit riders

Data provided by the NPS Assateague Island National Seashore. Map created by the Volpe Center and Tennessee Valley Authority.

Joint NPS/USFWS Jurisdiction
US FWS
NPS
NASA
Town of Chincoteague

Solutions not included on map: close Assateague Island to personal vehicles during peak hours during peak season (July and August weekends, 10am to 2pm); provide information on peak visitation times, options for beach access, and real-time parking information at hotels, campgrounds, and the Chamber of Commerce (also website, 800 number); implement special event and peak weekend traffic routing; modify existing Pony Express vehicles to add bicycle racks and accommodation for other gear.

Alternative 4: Eliminate all beach parking

Alternative 4 represents eliminating the beach parking lots entirely. This alternative includes a small number of High effort and cost transportation solutions intended to provide the highest level of improvements in safety, transit, bicycle and pedestrian features, especially as they relate to new off-site parking infrastructure. The latter is a real key to the long-term transportation system success at CNWR and in the Town of Chincoteague. Damage from the November 2009 nor'easter has shown that all of Assateague Island is vulnerable to major storm-related damages and that even reconfigured parking within CNWR is probably not sustainable.

The key new infrastructure and parking solution for Alternative 4 is a new parking structure (assumed capacity of 500 cars for estimating purposes) that would be High implementation effort and time, Very High cost (estimated $7.75M construction cost, plus high added annual O/M costs), and a controversial political challenge. The new garage would be served by permanent bus/shuttle transit extensions, using new vehicles, possibly burning an alternative fuel (two at $200,000 - $400,000 each). The garage and the shuttle service could both complement the satellite parking sites identified in Alternative 3 (total capacity – 455 cars). Thus the total off-site parking would be 955 cars. Higher total capacity would require a larger parking structure, whose capital and O/M costs would rise roughly proportionally with capacity. Figure Y4 shows a xxx-car garage of typical modern design.

Alternative 4 would complete bicycle access needs by providing shoulders on the Route 175 Causeway, at High effort, time, and cost ($2.8M).

All the transportation solutions of Alternatives 2 and 3 would still be in place, except those that explicitly address improvements at the existing lots and the widening of the Assateague Channel Bridge. The latter is a high impact, high-expense item needed to reduce congested automobile traffic, and therefore would be unnecessary given the strong traffic and parking management solutions that would accompany elimination of the beach parking lots. See Table 12. Map 23 is a map of the study area showing locations of the solutions.

More detailed descriptions of the alternatives' characteristics appear in Appendix F.

Table 12. Alternative 4.

	Transportation Solutions	Owner	Partners	Implement-ation	Time Frame	Political	Cost
Engineering/ Infrastructure	NONE						
Parking and Parking Management	Construct new parking structure off-site, probably in the Town of Chincoteague, with shuttle service to the beach.	CWNR/ASIS	None	HIGH	HIGH	HIGH	VERY HIGH
Bicycles and Pedestrians	Widen Route 175 causeway to provide shoulders for bicycle lanes and emergency vehicle access in both directions.	VDOT	Counnty, Town	HIGH	HIGH	HIGH	VERY HIGH
	Provide bike lanes along both sides of Maddox Blvd. to fill in gaps from Main Street to the Chamber of Commerce traffic circle (eliminate on-street parking).	VDOT	Town	HIGH	MEDIUM	MEDIUM	MEDIUM
Transit	Include the parking garage in Green route.	Pony Express or other service	CNWR/ASIS, Town	MEDIUM	MEDIUM	LOW	LOW
	Purchase new vehicles (2) for service to CNWR and ASIS sites. Should consider alternative fuel vehicle equipped with bicycle racks that can accommodate gear more easily.	Pony Express or other service	CNWR/ASIS, Town	HIGH	MEDIUM	LOW	HIGH

Map 23. Alternative 4 Solutions.

— — Route 175 Causeway: Widen to provide shoulders for bicycle lanes and emergency vehicle
access in both directions
▪▪▪▪▪ Maddox Boulevard: provide bicycle lanes along both sides (eliminate on-street parking)
1) Eliminate beach parking and construct parking garage somewhere on Chincoteague Island, to be
served by shuttle

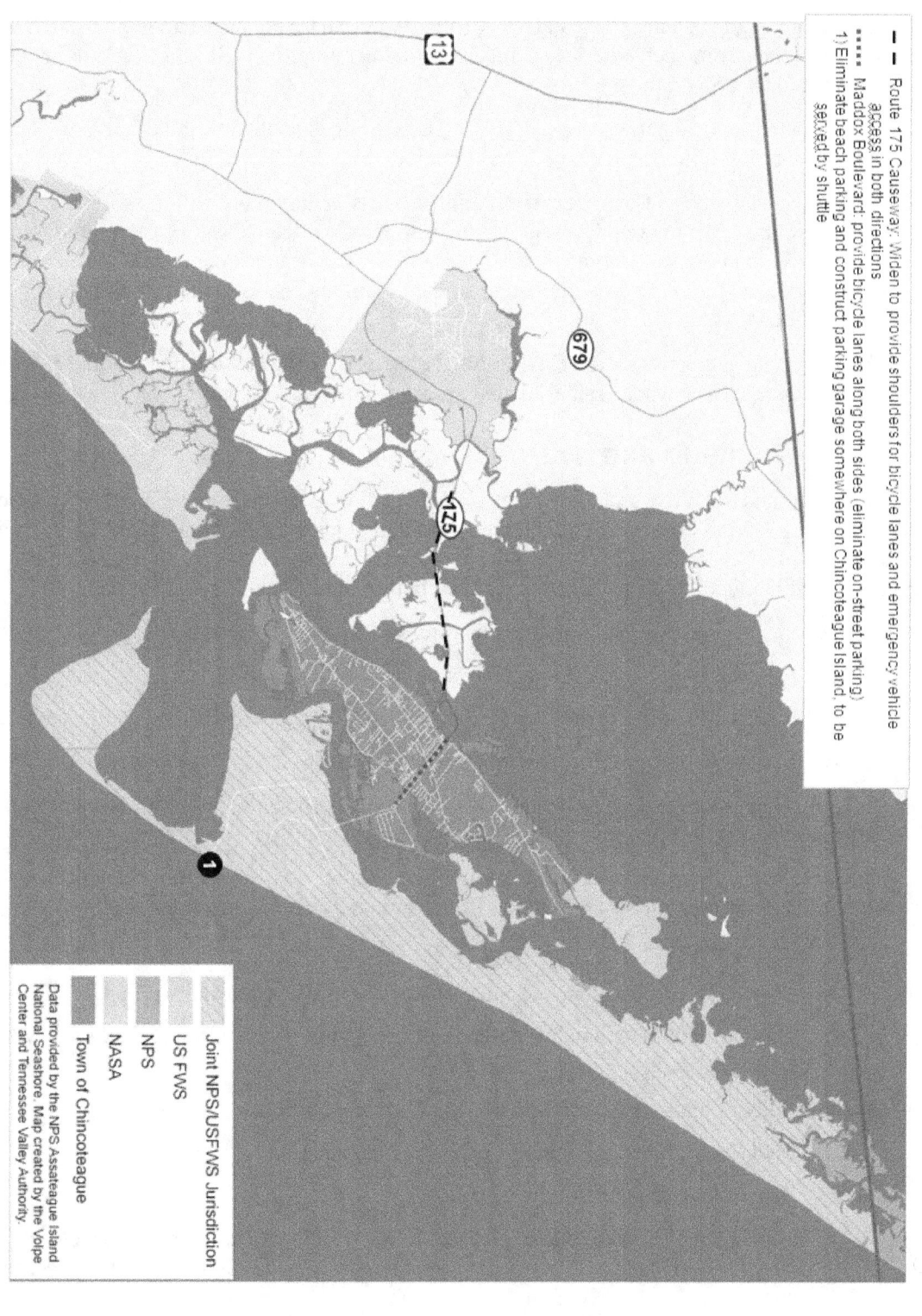

Joint NPS/USFWS Jurisdiction
US FWS
NPS
NASA
Town of Chincoteague

Data provided by the NPS Assateague Island
National Seashore. Map created by the Volpe
Center and Tennessee Valley Authority.

Solutions not included on map: include parking garage along Green Route of Pony Express; purchase new vehicles (2) for service to CNWR and ASIS sites – should consider alternative fuel vehicle equipped with bicycle racks and that can accommodate gear more easily.

7 Assessment of Solutions and Alternatives

The assessment of the transportation alternatives consisted of the following steps:

- Development of six consolidated assessment criteria. These are based upon goals of the NPS and the FWS; however, each criterion includes a particular emphasis relevant to this project, as articulated by CNWR.

- Development of a numeric scoring system. The scoring is applied for all criteria to the individual transportation solutions making up the alternatives.

- Scoring the solutions. The project team jointly discussed and scored all the solutions. The point of this exercise was to provide a relative measure for the effectiveness of the solutions, not necessarily to numerically compare the alternatives. The results are intended to be a useful guide for CNWR and the ATPPL co-applicants in their planning and execution of particular solutions in the coming years.

- Assessing the alternatives. The final result is a series of textual assessments of the alternatives, each considered as a whole, rather than aggregate comparative scores.

Assessment criteria and scoring

The Volpe Center and CNWR worked cooperatively to develop assessment criteria that reflect elements of both NPS and FWS missions, ATPPL program goals and guidance (including ATPPL), and the particular needs of CNWR, its ATPPL co-applicants, and residents and visitors. Elimination of redundancies and integration of similar items resulted in this consolidated set of criteria:

- Protection and conservation of natural, historic, and cultural resources;
    - o Reduced traffic volume and congestion in CNWR
    - o Reduced footprint of parking facilities in CNWR, particularly in sensitive resource areas
    - o Minimized physical and aesthetic (viewscape) impact of any transportation solutions

- Optimization of the transportation system's operational efficiency to improve visitor mobility, safety, and accessibility;
    - o Provision of transit service that effectively serves all of the Town of Chincoteague, with particular emphasis on Maddox Boulevard, and key destinations in CNWR
    - o Improved pedestrian/bicycle access to CNWR
    - o Improved pedestrian/bicycle safety on main approaches to and within CNWR
    - o Improvement of automobile safety on main approaches to CNWR, including Maddox Boulevard and the Route 175 Causeway

- Sustainability of transportation system, to minimize congestion and pollution
    - o Reduced traffic congestion in Town of Chincoteague
    - o Reduced parking pressure in CNWR
    - o Utilization of existing parking facilities and disturbed land to replace or relocate existing beach parking capacity, which is vulnerable to storms, shoreline change, and climate change

- Improvement of the visitor experience, in particular the understanding and appreciation of fish and wildlife resources;

- Improved access to CNWR resulting in enhanced visitor experience in uncongested conditions. The purpose of improved access is not to maximize visitation but to allow visitors to experience CNWR without extensive traffic delays and congested conditions.
- Improved visitor awareness/knowledge about CNWR and ASIS, through access to key sites within CNWR and ASIS, with opportunities for interpretation
- Improved experience for visitors traveling to and from the beach
- Improved visitor way finding

- Fostering and sustaining partnerships
  - Requirement for partnerships with municipal/county/state entities
  - Reinforcement of co-applicant planning goals (CNWR, ASIS, Town of Chincoteague, County, and A-NPDC)
  - Promotion of economic and social benefits from tourism

- Financial sustainability and cost-effectiveness
  - Minimization of operations and maintenance costs
  - Development of fare/fee structure that supports the costs of the transportation system

To develop the scoring approach, a "scoring rationale" was developed for each criterion to identify the "primary program element," or the most important sub-bullet, of each criterion as well as secondary considerations. The criteria were then assigned a scoring range of 1 to 5, with 1 indicating a negative impact to that criteria, 2 indicating no impact or not applicable, and 3-5 indicating increasingly positive impact. The last criterion, financial sustainability, was given slightly different definitions for each score. Table 13 below shows the scoring rationale, and explanation of the meaning of each numeric score for each criterion.

Table 13. Assessment Criteria for Transportation Alternatives.

Assessment Criteria	Protection and conservation of natural, historic, and cultural resources	Optimization of the transportation system's operational efficiency to improve visitor mobility, safety, and accessibility	Sustainability of transportation system, to minimize congestion and pollution	Improvement of the visitor experience, in particular the understanding and appreciation of fish and wildlife resources	Fostering and sustaining partnerships	Financial sustainability
Scoring Rationale	Natural resources are the main program element, followed by cultural/historic resources.	Safe multi-modal access to the Town and CNWR is the primary program element, followed by an effective transportation system that serves the Town and CNWR.	Reduced traffic congestion in Town and parking pressure in CNWR are the primary program element, followed by pollution effects	The educational component of a CNWR visitor's experience in CNWR and ASIS is the primary program element, followed by beachgoers' experience.	The partnerships with the ATPPL co-applicants, including the primary program element, followed by new or enhanced partnerships with other entities.	The emphasis is on control of O/M costs (long term financial burden), including the fare/fee structure. The capital cost component is less important; assume that funding sources are found. Scores represent probable outcomes.

Scoring Range		(Criteria)	Financial sustainability
	5	High positive impact - significant benefit for primary program element; may include other benefits as well	Lowest Financial burden; no annual O/M, possible costs at multi-year
	4	Moderate positive impact - some benefit for primary and other program elements; or significant benefit for non-primary elements	Low annual O/M costs; may be easily incorporated into existing activities
	3	Minor positive impact - no benefit for primary program element; minor benefit for non-primary elements	Moderate annual O/M costs; may require new procedures or activities by owner
	2	No impact or NA	High annual O/M costs; requiring new procedures or activities by owner
	1	Negative impact, particularly as regards the primary program element	Financially unsustainable

Assessment results

The Volpe Center project team assessed all alternatives, including Alternative 1 (No Action), in accordance with the criteria shown in Table 13. The summarized results appear as textual descriptions in subsections i through iv, for each criterion. The numeric scoring results appear in Appendix F. As mentioned above, the scoring and summaries are a result of project team discussions and are intended to provide relative rather than absolute measure for the effectiveness of the solutions. An explanation of the partnerships criterion and potential for partnerships will be further described in Chapter 8. The Volpe Center project team discussed and scored all the solutions, and these results were subsequently reviewed by FWS.

Alternative 1

Alternative 1 is the continuation of the status quo. The focus of the assessment is on shortcomings of the existing conditions, so by definition and with reference to Table 13, every item has either negative impact or no impact on the transportation system, with respect to all the assessment criteria.

- <u>Protection and conservation of natural, historic, and cultural resources.</u> The current dependence on private vehicles for access for the majority of visitors leads to tailpipe emissions and liquid spillage that impact natural resources in CNWR and ASIS. In addition, the location of the existing beach parking lots and their maintenance by ASIS reduce natural habitat for several endangered species, as well as many other migratory birds, and disrupts the natural westward progression of the beach.

- <u>Optimization of the transportation system's operational efficiency to improve visitor mobility, safety, and accessibility.</u> The existing transportation infrastructure has many shortcomings that contribute to safety problems, congestion and pollution, and inefficient multi-modal travel. Maddox Boulevard and Main Street, among other main roads in the Town of Chincoteague, lack consistent pavement markings for travel lanes, shoulders, and parking. The Assateague Channel Bridge lacks bypass capability to easily accommodate transit and emergency vehicles. Route 175 lacks shoulders, emergency pull-off areas, signage for the Queens Sound turn, speed control interventions, and real-time traffic monitoring. The public beach lacks emergency shelters and public notification system, exposing visitors to severe weather, especially those not using cars to access the beach.

  In addition, there are significant gaps in bike trails and lanes, in particular between the Town of Chincoteague and CNWR, as well as sidewalk gaps on main thoroughfares, and a lack of crosswalks and pedestrian signals at signalized intersections. All lead to unsafe conditions and are barriers to bicycle and pedestrian use, leading in turn to increased use of private automobiles and attendant congestion and pollution.

  Finally, the existing trolley service does not carry passengers to CNWR and the vehicles do not accommodate bicycles or other recreational gear. The trolley service also does not offer temporary alternative access to the beach when beach lot capacity is reduced or when lots are full. Consequently, it does not mitigate beach traffic congestion and pollution and does not facilitate bicycle use within CNWR for those who do not feel comfortable bicycling from the Town to CNWR. In addition, the current transit routes overlap and are long and circuitous and may not be providing a service that attracts all potential riders.

- <u>Sustainability of transportation system, to minimize congestion and pollution.</u> There is a an overall lack of simple, low-cost provision of information, including real-time traffic and parking information, pre-trip planning, and off-site pre-purchasing of passes. This lack causes or exacerbates fee booth delays, peak day traffic congestion, and parking shortages, which in turn result in pollution and visitor inconvenience and frustration.

- **Improvement of the visitor experience, in particular the understanding and appreciation of fish and wildlife resources**. Current transportation conditions do not allow all visitors, including those who are mobility-impaired, to easily access resources, in particular by bicycling or walking, nor does it effectively provide interpretative and educational services in CNWR.

- **Fostering and sustaining partnerships**. The conditions described in this assessment limit opportunities for fostering and sustaining partnerships for CNWR and its co-applicants. Failure to improve transportation infrastructure, traveler information, and multi-modal transport options is detrimental to other attractions and businesses in the area, because of wasted travel time and visitor frustration.

- **Financial sustainability**. The unpaved parking lots at the public beach sustain storm damage frequently and as a result require costly annual maintenance and repairs; in addition, the long-term physical survival of these lots is questionable because of ongoing and accelerating shoreline changes. The lack of designated off-site beach parking leaves visitors with no alternative parking options during summer peak days or when beach lot capacity is reduced due to severe weather and also limits the potential of transit service into CNWR since visitors either wait in queue outside the CNWR fee booths or disperse to many locations in the Town of Chincoteague.

Alternative 2

The transportation solutions in Alternative 2 are low-cost, quickly implementable improvements to the status quo, wherein the beach parking lots remain in their current configuration and visitation exceeds capacity ten to twenty days per year. The solutions mainly address traffic congestion, safety (especially for bicyclists and pedestrians), and improved information for travelers, without significant infrastructure or operational solutions for parking.

- **Protection and conservation of natural, historic, and cultural resources**. Most solutions represent a limited promotion of transportation alternatives to personal cars and improvements to traffic operations that would result in modest reductions in congestion, tailpipe emissions, and liquid spillage affecting CNWR. Constructing a bicycle trail between the Assateague Channel Bridge and the Chamber of Commerce traffic circle would enhance bicycle travel and have a significant positive effect.

- **Optimization of the transportation system's operational efficiency to improve visitor mobility, safety, and accessibility**. Several infrastructure solutions directly address improvement of safety (particularly on the Route 175 Causeway), and many other traffic and parking management measures improve mobility and accessibility, with modest benefits for safety. The siren notification system at the beach would be a significant safety improvement.

- **Sustainability of transportation system, to minimize congestion and pollution**. Limited promotion of transportation alternatives to personal cars and improvements to traffic operations result in modest reductions in congestion, tailpipe emissions, and liquid spillage affecting the greater project area.

- **Improvement of the visitor experience, in particular the understanding and appreciation of fish and wildlife resources**. Several of the safety focus items do not affect the visitor experience. Several traffic and parking management measures items add to the convenience of information retrieval, purchases of passes, and entry into CNWR, with modest effect upon the visitor experience. The enhanced information and improved access promote visits to non-beach sites in CNWR. The bicycle path and mobility-impaired access improvements should result in significant visitor experience improvements. The pilot transit service to CNWR improves shoulder season access to CNWR and ASIS resources and may provide an opportunity for some on-board interpretative services.

- Fostering and sustaining partnerships. This alternative includes solutions that share information and promote alternative transportation. In particular, the transit route extension into CNWR, have strong partnership potential among many entities.

- Financial sustainability. These solutions are mainly low-cost items; most have negligible to low annual operations and maintenance (O/M) cost burden. It should, however, be noted that the solutions in this alternative do not decrease the status quo cost of maintaining the existing beach parking lots.

Alternative 3

This alternative includes the largest group of solutions with significant positive effect, including three important engineering and infrastructure measures for improved safety, five important traffic management measures (four of which are ITS), and two parking management measures including the full implementation of satellite parking. The transportation solutions added in Alternative 3 represent longer-term, significant commitments to providing a transportation system to move visitors between off-site parking facilities and the public beach, along with key improvements in safety and traffic management. The solutions mainly address safety, alternative parking and improved bicycle access that would reduce traffic congestion, parking demand, and pollution within the study area.

- Protection and conservation of natural, historic, and cultural resources. In all, Alternative 3 represents a systematized program, to provide alternative parking and reduce traffic and pollution in CNWR, that would overall have a significant positive impact, although some individual solutions may have negative impacts.

  There are several parking management solutions designed to reduce traffic and parking in a way that would benefit the resources. In addition to a significant ITS measure to provide real-time beach parking status information to travelers and an operational measure to restrict beach access during summer peak hours, there is the designation of satellite parking at existing community and public lots (Chincoteague Center and Town Hall, the High School, and the Elementary School) for peak seasonal beach parking, to be serviced by a shuttle. Construction of a new trail between the Black Duck trail and the beach for bicycle and pedestrian access would also significantly reduce vehicle traffic into CNWR.

  However, the engineering and infrastructure solutions for safety and emergency response on the Route 175 Causeway and the CNWR fee booth relocation may have negative impacts on the natural resources due to construction that would infringe upon undeveloped areas. The traffic management solutions in this alternative are modest in scale and effect.

- Optimization of the transportation system's operational efficiency to improve visitor mobility, safety, and accessibility. This alternative includes the largest group of solutions with significant positive effect, including three important engineering and infrastructure measures for improved safety, five important traffic management measures (four of which are ITS), and two parking management measures including the full implementation of satellite parking.

  The infrastructure solutions are emergency shelters on the beach, reconfiguration of the Assateague Channel Bridge to provide an express lane into CNWR for transit and emergency vehicle access, addition of a bicycle/pedestrian bridge adjacent to the Assateague Channel Bridge, and shoulders and additional emergency pull-off areas on the Route 175 Causeway, all of which have significant safety benefits. The latter two enhance transit and bicycle access as well.

The traffic management solutions, both individually and collectively, have significant positive impact. Relocating the CNWR fee booths further east from the Assateague Channel Bridge would provide additional storage capacity for queuing vehicles and accommodate an express lane for transit vehicles and pre-paid cars. The ITS solutions would provide real-time beach parking and traffic information via variable message signs and a website, detailed information for visitors on peak visitation times and options for beach access, and special event and peak weekend traffic routing via variable message signs and/or traffic signal timing. Access to this information gives visitors the opportunity to avoid problems and make better traveling and parking choices, thus reducing congestion. Cameras to monitor traffic on the Route 175 Causeway would improve safety through better incident management.

The most important parking management solution is the designation of existing community and public parking lots for peak seasonal beach parking, to be serviced by shuttle buses. It is the most effective short-term solution, as it quickly increases capacity without any new infrastructure. The capacity in these lots can and should be a part of any effort to address parking, including the construction of an off-site parking garage, as seen in Alternative 4.

The bike trail (in CNWR) and pedestrian safety measures (in Town) have significant positive impact because of anticipated inducement for more people to use those travel modes.

The transit routing additions and new gear and bicycle accommodations on the vehicles will greatly expand visitor access options, both in to CNWR and around the Town of Chincoteague. This expansion would serve both day trippers who are parking off-site and longer term visitors staying at hotels, motels, and campgrounds in the Town of Chincoteague.

- Sustainability of transportation system, to minimize congestion and pollution. In tandem with the positive impact on the transportation system optimization, Alternative 3 also has high positive impact for peak-time reductions of congestion and pollution. This is mostly due to the parking management solutions, especially satellite parking, in concert with ITS solutions making better information available to travelers and transit solutions linking the new parking options to CNWR.

  Specifically, the infrastructure measures have minor impact, only outside the CNWR, and the traffic management measures will reduce CNWR vehicle use only slightly. The parking management measures, except for satellite parking, are expected to have low impacts. The bike trail and pedestrian safety solutions in Chincoteague have modest positive effects, again because of anticipated inducement for more people to use those travel modes.

- Improvement of the visitor experience, in particular the understanding and appreciation of fish and wildlife resources. The infrastructure, parking, and traffic measures will bring mostly modest improvements to visitor experience, through improved convenience and reduced frustration. The bicycle and pedestrian solutions will allow and encourage more visitors to get close to CNWR's many resources. The transit service to CNWR would provide a unique opportunity for interpretive services on the vehicles. The beach concessions identified in Alternative for bicyclists and pedestrians also appear here as an amenity available to transit riders.

- Fostering and sustaining partnerships. Several significant ITS and off-site visitor information solutions will require both new partnerships and enhancements of existing partnerships with the Town and several of its businesses to make the solutions work most effectively. The designation of satellite parking lots served by shuttle buses would require significant new partnership, including coordination and partnership with co-applicants, notably the Town and the County, the Pony Express or other service provider, and other stakeholders.

- Financial sustainability. For ASIS/CNWR, the relocation or size reduction of beach parking lots would likely reduce O/M and capital replacement costs significantly. Otherwise, the overall effect would be to add O/M effort and costs for new infrastructure (shelters, widened bridge, and new trail) and features of the ITS program. The Assateague Channel Bridge widening would require capital funding estimated at nearly $7M.

  The parking management solutions have low start-up costs and low O/M costs. Satellite parking will entail personnel and other operating costs, but will generate offsetting revenue.

  Bike and pedestrian routing and safety solutions in the Town of Chincoteague would total to nearly $200,000 in capital cost, but the incremental O/M would be minor, as they do not represent new types of public works maintenance operations. The extended bus route would add significant O/M costs for the operator including vehicle wear and tear, additional fuel and labor.

Alternative 4

Alternative 4 comprises only five transportation solutions, four of which are high capital cost items, that build upon new systems and initiatives put in place in Alternatives 2 and 3, for the scenario in which the beach parking lots are eliminated altogether. Notable among these is the construction of a new, off-site parking garage, at a suitable site to be determined in the Town of Chincoteague. Two other solutions provide for bike lanes on major roads (Route 175 Causeway and Maddox Boulevard). Transit service would be expanded to include the new parking garage and the fleet would be updated by the purchase of new vehicles built to accommodate beachgoers and possibly powered by an alternative fuel.

- Protection and conservation of natural, historic, and cultural resources. The parking garage is seen as a significant positive impact, to the extent that it facilitates elimination, or at least significant reduction, of the beach parking lots, which would be a real, positive reduction of the human footprint in a very sensitive environment and habitat; however, its location and construction would have to be carefully considered to avoid negative impacts elsewhere.

  Widening of the Route 175 Causeway would involve significant environmental impact to Wallops Neck and the Wire Narrows and Black Narrows Salt Marshes. The Maddox Boulevard bike lane work would have neutral impact and the transit improvements contribute modest beneficial effect as they would contribute to elimination of the beach parking lots.

- Optimization of the transportation system's operational efficiency to improve visitor mobility, safety, and accessibility. All solutions have some degree of positive impact. Widening the Route 175 Causeway would be a significant safety enhancement, as well as an alternative transportation asset for bicycles.

  The garage and associated transit service, in concert with the parking and transit solutions of Alternative 3, make up the integrated transportation system that is required to accommodate a new beach parking management strategy. These solutions provide for peak demand transportation to the beach and enhance accessibility.

- Sustainability of transportation system, to minimize congestion and pollution. Again, these solutions build upon those in Alternative 3 to reduce vehicle miles traveled, congestion, and the related pollution, especially in ASIS/CNWR.

  The two bike lane solutions have significant impact as well. Completion of the Maddox Boulevard lane would effectively tie together the local routes in the Town and in CNWR. The new bike route on the Route 175 Causeway would be an entirely new extension of that mode, providing attractive, safe access for bicyclists able and willing to come from the mainland.

- Improvement of the visitor experience, in particular the understanding and appreciation of fish and wildlife resources. These solutions have a significant positive impact by increasing the number of people taking transit to CNWR and ASIS and therefore increasing the possibility for them to experience interpretive services onboard. In addition, the Maddox Boulevard bike lanes significantly enhance access to ASIS/CNWR by that mode and so will bring more visitors close to many attractions in the Town of Chincoteague.

- Fostering and sustaining partnerships. These parking management and transit solutions will require building significantly upon the partnerships required for Alternative 3. The parking garage and satellite parking lots would both be served by shuttle buses, requiring additional coordination and partnership with co-applicants, notably the Town and the County, the Pony Express or other service provider, and other stakeholders.

- Financial sustainability. For ASIS/CNWR, the elimination of beach parking lots would certainly reduce O/M significantly.

The new parking garage would have very high start-up and capital costs (estimated at $7.75M) and high associated O/M costs (estimated at $342Kper year based on $684 per space). Capital expense would presumably be provided in budgets and grants, and the high running costs would be offset to some degree by parking revenue (68,400 cars @ $5 per vehicle would be the break-even point). However, in this alternative a new Assateague Channel Bridge is not required. The Route 175 Causeway widening is also capital-intensive (estimated at $2.8M); however, the incremental O/M costs would be a minor increase for VDOT maintenance.

The bike routing solutions in the Town of Chincoteague would be a modest capital cost (estimate: $25,000), and the incremental O/M would also be minor, as it would not represent a new type of public works maintenance.

The bus service to the parking garage would not add significant O/M costs for the operator. Two new vehicles would be fairly costly ($200-400,000 each), and the O/M costs for alternative vehicles would likely rise significantly to accommodate the new technology. However, the extended and improved service would be likely to induce increased ridership and offsetting revenues.

Detailed scoring of all transportation solutions and additional commentary appear in Appendix F.

8 Partnership Assessment

Effective alternative transportation solutions depend on partnerships between regional and local entities for the resources needed to plan, implement, and sustain them. This was clearly recognized in the 1997 Memorandum of Understanding between the U.S. Department of Interior and U.S. Department of Transportation, which set forth general terms and conditions for cooperatively developing and integrating transportation planning so as to improve public transportation in the National Parks. . Local governments, civic groups and regional organizations may identify goals and objectives for tourism, conservation, and mobility that overlap and complement the goals of a public lands unit. Working with these groups is important for successful implementation of projects and activities identified by and for the public lands unit.

The transportation alternatives for this study (Chapter 6) identified appropriate and effective short and long-term transportation solutions that CNWR, the co-applicants, and other key entities may implement in the future. The tables in Chapter 6 indicate that for nearly all of these solutions partner involvement is necessary for effective and efficient implementation. This chapter documents existing partnerships among CNWR, its co-applicants, and local and regional entities, and identifies and assesses opportunities for new partnerships or partner activities that would support the identified transportation solutions.

Approach

The partnership assessment consisted of the following tasks:

- Identification of existing and potential partners in consultation with CNWR (Chapter 2 describes co-applicants and stakeholders)

- Assessment of partner characteristics, including organizational goals, historic relationship with CNWR and co-applicants, and types of support

- Analysis of Partners and Solutions, organized by the categories of solutions presented in Chapter 6, with suggestions for partners to support each transportation solution.

CNWR and its co-applicants already have in place many elements of successful alternative transportation partnerships. Such elements were generically identified in a 2003 Volpe Center report, Partnering for Success: Techniques for Working with Partners to Plan for Alternative Transportation In National Park Service Units:

- Coordinate park-oriented alternative transportation system planning with other community needs.

- Involve NPS staff with community organizations

- Use public workshops and other gatherings to seek public input and generate support

- Include a wide spectrum of partners

- Seek out expertise and resources necessary to build knowledge and support.

- Use formal partnership devices to cement collaborative relationships.

- Provide financial or other incentives to encourage public participation.

- Use advocacy tools to build a support network.

For example, CNWR regularly fosters communication and collaboration with local partners, notably through a monthly "Community Leaders" meeting where CNWR and ASIS staff meet with invited key stakeholders. Invitees include elected officials from the Town of Chincoteague including the Mayor, U.S.

Congresspersons or their staff, the Accomack County supervisor, director of the Chamber of Commerce, and leaders of other civic and business organizations.

However, there are areas in which CNWR and its co-applicants can enhance their partnerships.

Partnerships can provide CNWR with a number of resources, including:

- Funding (directly or indirectly through grants or programs for which CNWR/ASIS are not eligible)

- In-kind support (staff, facilities, technical expertise)

- Capital (vehicles, equipment, facilities)

- Promotion and information dissemination (media, advertising, letters of support, community organization)

- Consensus/buy-in/political support.

Transportation goals that could be accomplished through partnerships identified in this chapter include:

- Disseminate traveler information

- Increase opportunities for funding and regional coordination

- Reduce congestion and parking delays on Refuge

- Improved traveler information, including electronic formats such as websites

- Increased alternative transportation use

- Improved visitor safety services

Finally, enhanced visitor experience is an important shared goal of the partners that, though not directly related to transportation, can be significantly affected by the safety, efficiency, and choice provided by the transportation system.

Existing Partnerships

CNWR already has several existing partnerships in place – beyond those with its co-applicants – that involve the following types of partnership activities:

- <u>Funding and In-Kind Support</u>. Activities include annual donations and volunteer services provided to CNWR.

- <u>Outreach and Information</u>. Services include media promotion, emergency information dissemination, distribution of brochures and outdoor advertising displays.

- <u>Interpretive and Educational Services.</u> Activities involve the provision of services by CNWR and ASIS to students, visitors and the general public.

- <u>Contractual Agreement</u>. Activities identified under or managed by a formal, written document.

These partners and activities were identified through consultation with CNWR and are summarized in Table 14. Co-applicants of this study (ASIS, Town of Chincoteague, Accomack County, and the Accomack-Northampton Planning Disctrict Commission) are not included as their relationships have been described previously.

Table 14. Current Partnerships.

Organization	Type of Activities	Details
Chincoteague Chamber of Commerce	Funding, Outreach and Information	• Annual donation • Lists CNWR and Chincoteague attractions and events on website
Chincoteague Natural History Association (CNHA)	Funding, In-Kind Support, Contractual Agreement	• Cooperating Association for CNWR.[52] • Operates wildlife bus tour and gift shop at CNWR • Produces and provides interpretive and educational material for CNWR visitors • All funds raised used to support and enhance interpretive programs, projects, and activities at CNWR
Chincoteague Volunteer Fire Company	In-Kind Support, Contractual Agreement	• Provides all fire services for Chincoteague and Assateague Islands • Owners of Chincoteague ponies, which graze on Assateague Island under a Special Use Permit with FWS and are governed by CNWR's Pony Management Plan
U.S. Coast Guard	In-Kind Support	• Patrol and enforcement of adjacent marine areas
WCTG 96.5 FM	Outreach and Information	• Makes announcements regarding Chincoteague and CNWR events • Interviewed CNWR Refuge Manager regarding the study and storm events in 2009
Beacon	Outreach and Information	• Publishes CNWR-related announcements and news
Eastern Shore Post	Outreach and Information	• Publishes CNWR-related announcements and news
Virginia Tourism Commission	Outreach and Information	• Provides information for various Chincoteague amenities as well as ASIS and CNWR on website and at Route 13 Welcome Center • Also hosts CNWR outdoor display at Route 13 Welcome Center
Eastern Shore Chamber of Commerce	Outreach and Information	• Lists CNWR events on online calendar
Eastern Shore Tourism Commission	Outreach and Information	• Lists CNWR events on online calendar

---

[52] National Wildlife Refuge Support Groups Program (Friends): Cooperating Associations. http://www fws.gov/friends/CoopAssoc/Default.asp

Table 14 (continued). Current Partnerships.

Organization	Type of Activities	Details
SPARK (Shore People Advancing Readiness for Knowledge)[53]	Interpretive/ Educational Use	• Uses CNWR as destination for Family Learning/Family Fun (FLFF) Days, attended by participating families
NASA Wallops Flight Facility	Interpretive/Educational Use	• CNWR/ASIS allows public to watch launches from beach (even when during non-operating hours)
Marine Science Consortium	Interpretive/Educational Use	• Uses CNWR/ASIS as resource for students

Potential Transportation Partners and Partnership Activities

As CNWR and its co-applicants implement appropriate transportation solutions identified by the assessment in Chapter 7, new and enhanced partnership activities with existing and new transportation partners will be required for the success of the solutions. This section identifies and discusses potential partners and activities for each category of solutions presented in Chapter 6, and then assesses and describes each partner and potential activities. References will be made to the categories of solutions presented in Chapter 6 as well as the categories of funding, marine transportation, and safety and emergency management. Safety and emergency management is integrated into other categorical solutions but merits particular mention because of their programmatic importance to CNWR and its co-applicants.

Partnership Opportunities by Category of Solutions

1. *Engineering/infrastructure.*

VDOT, Accomack County, A-NPDC, and the Town of Chincoteague are responsible for engineering and infrastructure solutions in terms of planning, funding, and implementation. The County and Town provide oversight within their respective jurisdictions. The inclusion and endorsement of major capital projects in regional transportation plans will help the likelihood of such projects gaining approval and funding, particularly those that address safety improvements in the study area.

2. *Traffic management*

Traffic management solutions require engagement of the VDOT, Accomack County, A-NPDC, and the Town of Chincoteague. These solutions also require technical expertise for operating and maintaining intelligent transportation systems. Additional partners for disseminating traveler information and providing the off-site sale of passes are also required. Those partners already engaged in the dissemination of information on CNWR and ASIS attractions and events could easily modify their brochures, flyers, and websites to add traveler information, such as peak visitation times and alternative modes to access the beach. Real-time information, such as parking availability and traffic back-ups, may also be distributed using existing information outlets such as websites.

3. *Parking and parking management*

Parking and parking management solutions include several infrastructure and operational improvements at the beach, ITS and information sharing processes, satellite parking areas, and the construction of a

---

[53] http://www.sparkfamilies.org/

parking garage. Owners of potential satellite parking areas, namely the Accomack County Public Schools and the Town of Chincoteague, are important partners. In addition, some entities, such as the Town, may be interested in partnering with CNWR to construct a parking garage. As the Town considers eliminating parking on Maddox Boulevard, it will be necessary to provide off-street parking.

4. *Bicycle and pedestrian improvements*

Key partners to engage in bicycle and pedestrian improvements include the Town of Chincoteague, VDOT, private bicycle outfitters, and interpretive and cultural institutions, such as CNHA and the Oyster and Maritime Museum. On the regional scale, the County and A-NPDC and VDOT could provide support of a regional bicycle system. Locally, the Town could promote bicycling through an improved map, signage, educational campaign, and infrastructure improvements in partnership with VDOT, which owns the roads. Bicycle outfitters could provide promotional and financial support for education, and wayfinding and infrastructure improvements such as bicycle parking and lockers at the beach as well as conducting bicycle tours. Interpretive entities could offer cultural and historic walking and bicycle tours, such as between the Oyster and Maritime Museum and the Lighthouse. On the regional scale, the County and A-NPDC and VDOT could provide support for a regional bicycle system.

5. *Transit*

Transit partners could support new and reconfigured routes and services and assist in providing additional transit vehicles. Two national examples of transit systems that have resulted from extensive partnerships with state, local, and NPS units are Acadia National Park's Island Explorer system and Cape Cod Rural Transit Authority's Flex system. There are several other examples of private partnerships in which a concessionaire operates a transportation service (ferry or bus primarily) that serves the public lands unit.

Four local entities that currently provide transit and may be able to assist in the implementation of future transit include:

- Town of Chincoteague's Pony Express
- CNHA
- STAR Transit
- Accomack County Public Schools

The involvement of state and Federal entities, namely the Virginia Department of Rail and Public Transportation and the Federal Transit Administration, is important for obtaining both funding and regulatory approval. Several other entities were identified that could provide assistance with interpretive services (e.g., tour guides), audio tours, or visitor assistance in loading gear onto the bus (e.g., youth employment). Finally, all of the entities identified as outlets for traveler information could also provide information on transit services.

Town of Chincoteague

The involvement of the Town of Chincoteague is essential to the success of many of the solutions, in part because many of the solutions occur within the Town's jurisdiction and/or require Town resources. In particular, Town partnership is invaluable for those solutions involving pedestrian and bicycle improvements, traffic management, and the provision of off-site parking and transit to the beach and other CNWR sites.

The Town's structure includes several entities and individuals that have particular relevance to transportation. The Town Planner is an important contact who can help coordinate between the various regional entities and identify opportunities for investment and funding. The Recreation and Community Enhancement Committee can continue its recent work on updating the bicycle plan, identifying bicycle investments, disseminating educational materials on bicycling etiquette, and reapplying for Safe Routes to Schools and other funding sources. The Chincoteague Police Department could provide traffic control.

In the short-term, the Town of Chincoteague could offer weekend satellite parking in the Town Hall parking for shuttles to serve. The Town of Chincoteague can also work with DRPT, FTA, and CNWR to propose the use of the Pony Express for emergency storm events, regular service to CNWR, and weekend-only service to the beach. The current trolleys are only used during the evenings, so they would be available for new or expanded daytime service.

In the long-term, the Town of Chincoteague could be a key partner in the construction of a parking garage. The Town of Chincoteague's Comprehensive Plan (2009) identifies the need to explore a parking garage in downtown. These factors indicate a willingness and interest to consider a parking garage within Chincoteague that could match CNWR's interest in providing at least some parking off-site from the beach.

Finally, if a marine solution were to be explored further, the Town of Chincoteague has ownership of the East Side Road dock and parking facilities that were identified as the best candidate for an origin site for service to the Assateague Lighthouse.

Accomack County Public Schools

Accomack County Public Schools could provide use of the parking areas at the high school and elementary school under an agreement through the Town or directly with CNWR. The Schools, which have their own transportation fleet, could also provide driver and maintenance support to any expanded or new transit service.

Accomack County and Accomack-Northampton Planning District Commission (A-NPDC)

Both Accomack County and Accomack-Northampton Planning District oversee regional plans and initiatives, such as the Eastern Shore of Virginia Bicycle Plan and 2035 Long-Range Transportation Plan, which feed into state plans and help identify projects to receive funding from state and other sources. The two entities also can provide technical assistance to local jurisdictions, such as the Town of Chincoteague, for planning for and implementing transportation projects.

Other Regional Entities

Accomack and Northampton counties lie between two other established areas: Maryland's Eastern Shore and Hampton Roads. Despite being part of VDOT's Hampton Roads District (District 5), neither Accomack nor Northampton Counties or their respective towns are included in the Hampton Roads Partnership, a group of counties and cities to the south of Virginia's Eastern Shore that have been actively involved in regional transportation planning, including transit planning. Connecting with this entity, or similar entities in Maryland, could increase the region's ability to access resources and introduce innovative solutions.

Virginia Department of Transportation (VDOT)

VDOT is a key partner in the future of transportation for CNWR and its co-applicants because of its roles as owner of all major roads in the study area, clearinghouse for technical assistance, and gatekeeper to planning processes essential for funding.

VDOT is responsible for the Statewide Transportation Improvement Program (STIP), a four-year document that identifies those highway construction and maintenance and transit projects that will utilize federal funding, or for which federal approval will be required. It is also the document that identifies the project scheduling dates for transportation projects and programs. The STIP includes approved Transportation Improvement Programs (TIPs) from the designated metropolitan planning organization

(MPO) areas in the state as well as all federally-funded highway projects located outside the MPO areas. Projects funded under the Federal Highway Administration's Office of Federal Lands Highway programs are also included along with those projects to improve park roads and parkways found within the federal parks in Virginia.

VDOT works in partnership with A-NDPC to identify capital transportation projects within the region to place on the STIP. VDOT can work with CNWR and its co-applicants, in particular Accomack County and A-NDPC, to include transportation projects identified in previous studies, this study, and in the future that benefit the region.

VDOT can also offer assistance to CNWR and its co-applicants in terms of traffic and speeding data collection, safety analyses, and the funding and staffing, or contracting, of specific transportation studies and projects for the study area. VDOT can assess and help implement the recommendations from the Route 13 / Wallops Island Access Study and Chincoteague 2020 Transportation Plan. VDOT can also conduct a study of impacts of the new Route 175 bridge alignment on traffic within Chincoteague.

Although currently there is no ITS deployed on Virginia's Eastern Shore, future installation and monitoring of such systems, such as traffic cameras and VMS on Route 13 and Route 175, could be conducted by VDOT's Hampton Roads Traffic Operations Center.

Virginia Department of Rail and Public Transit (DRPT)

DRPT provides funding and oversight for public transportation in Virginia, including STAR Transit and Pony Express. Any modification to the existing service of the Pony Express or new public transportation service would require DRPT approval and coordination with FTA through DRPT.

The DRPT's Six-Year Improvement Plan (SYIP) includes funding for public transportation facilities and programs, commuter programs, and all interstate and primary highway projects that are being studied, designed, and constructed throughout Virginia over six fiscal years. The Commonwealth Transportation Board (CTB), a 17-member board appointed by the Governor, updates the program each year as priorities are revised, project schedules and costs change, and study results are known. All projects in the SYIP that are eligible for federal funding will be included in the DRPT Statewide Transportation Improvement Plan (STIP), a separate document from the STIP described above. The Town of Chincoteague's Pony Express operations and capital funding is including in both the current SYIP and DRPT STIP. Any future public transportation projects would also need to be listed in these documents.

DRPT is the state sponsor for Try Transit Week, a statewide event focused on promoting the use of transit that so far has occurred in September of 2008 and 2009 and is being planned for 2010. Virginians pledge online and are entered into a drawing for a one-year free transit pass for the transit system of the winner's choice. The website contains a directory of transit options available by region; STAR Transit is included but Pony Express is not. The Town of Chincoteague and partners could get involved in this event for both STAR Transit and the Pony Express and this event could be instrumental in introducing and encouraging transit connection to CNWR and ASIS.

Other State Agencies

Two other state agencies that may be important to consider engaging are the Virginia Department of Emergency Management (DEM) and the Virginia Department of Environmental Quality (DEQ). DEM is a possible partner in the terms of support and funding for safety improvements, in particular provision adding lanes and widening streets for emergency vehicle access, installing beach siren notification system, and constructing beach shelters. The DEQ, through the Virginia Coastal Zone Management Program is invested in the Seaside Water Trail and would be interested in any promotion of non-motorized water access and the provision of relevant marine infrastructure.

Local Media

The local newspapers, the Chincoteague Beacon and the Eastern Shore Post, could increase coverage of transportation conditions within Chincoteague and CNWR and ASIS, in particular providing static traveler information, such as peak visitation times to the beach and alternative modes to access the beach. The Chincoteague Beacon has a good history of covering important local issues and Eastern Shore Post showed interest in covering transportation issues by sending a reporter to one of the study's public meetings. The local radio station, WCTG 96.5 FM, could provide similar information but also provide real-time updates on parking availability, traffic backup, beach or weather safety concerns and general conditions, as well as preannounced interviews with representatives of the co-applicants to discuss transportation issues and conditions. The radio station manager has shown and expressed interest in formalizing this role.

Transportation Service Partners

The Town of Chincoteague's Pony Express and the Accomack County Public Schools are both key transportation providers. STAR Transit, the regional public transportation provider for Accomack and Northampton counties, could undertake a number of activities to assist in improving public transportation in and around Chincoteague. Its vehicles are already mandated to be available for an evacuation and are also available on weekends. STAR Transit could coordinate its scheduling and route design with the Pony Express and any new service. It could also provide vehicle replacement, maintenance, and driver support for existing, expanded, or new transit service.

For marine transportation, the Chincoteague Island Charter Boat Association and its members could operate services between Chincoteague and Assateague Islands under concessionaire or special use permits.

Civic and Business Associations

All of the civic, tourism and business associations can host static travel information, such as peak visitation times to the beach and alternative modes to access the beach, on their websites. Some of these entities with physical public destinations, such as the Chincoteague Chamber of Commerce and Virginia Tourism Commission, could also provide off-site pass sales and posting of real-time information on traffic conditions.

Private Businesses

Private businesses are important partners to consider. Any local or regional business represents a potential client for advertising or sponsoring some aspect of the transportation system, such as bicycle parking. Some private entities in particular, namely hotels and other lodging businesses and bicycle and other alternative transportation rental companies, may have more vested interest in providing easy access to bicycles and bicycle amenities, such as maps, guided tours, parking, and lockers. These same entities could provide travel information to guests and users along with promotional and educational materials about bicycling. Other private entities with cultural and educational missions, such as the Oyster and Maritime Museum and CNHA, could provide interpretive audio tours or transit or walking tours by volunteers from Chincoteague to Assateague Island.

9 Findings and Next Steps

FWS and NPS missions define the paramount goals of resource protection, visitor experience, and financial sustainability. The ASIS and CNWR planning and management processes include an assessment of the sustainability of the public beach parking lots, which are located directly adjacent to the ocean beach, occupy important wildlife habitat, and frequently sustain serious storm and wave damage requiring expensive repairs. The management of beach parking is the key driver for the transportation analysis in this study.

The transportation solutions identified herein enhance wildlife values, access and safety, and the visitor experience. Combinations of these solutions form transportation alternatives, the objectives of which are to reduce traffic congestion, facilitate the formation and operation of alternative transportation, and improve emergency management and transportation safety, while minimizing transportation's adverse effects on the natural environment. Key planning documents for the Town of Chincoteague and Accomack County specify similar transportation planning objectives and so are also addressed by these alternatives.

a. Assessment of alternatives

The four alternatives include a "no action" alternative and three action alternatives that address CNWR and ASIS program needs, particularly natural resources and visitor experience, and the transportation needs of the other ATPPL co-applicants: the Town of Chincoteague, Accomack County, and the Accomack–Northampton Planning District Commission.

Alternative 1 (No Action)

The existing transportation system has evolved in response to peak visitation conditions that occur during summer holidays and weekends and the ASIS/CNWR policy that has maintained parking at the public beach for 961 automobiles, at significant annual expense. The ATPPL co-applicants, along with VDOT, have developed good planning tools and made progress toward improving access, safety, and transportation options within the study area; however, there are still significant gaps, particularly when one considers future scenarios with reduced or non-existent beach parking. The key status quo conditions and concerns are the following:

- Road infrastructure. Major roads providing access to CNWR lack shoulders, emergency pull-off areas, speed control interventions (Route 175 Causeway) and consistent pavement markings to indicate travel lanes, shoulders, and parking (Maddox Boulevard and Main Street). These give rise to safety concerns for ASIS/CNWR, VDOT and the Town of Chincoteague and hinder safe, efficient multi-modal travel, especially for bicycles.

  The Assateague Channel Bridge lacks bypass capability to accommodate transit and emergency vehicles. Emergency response delays during congested conditions are a safety concern for CNWR.

- Emergency response. There are no shelters or siren notification system on the beach for emergency evacuation and storm warnings. The safety concern is exposure of visitors to severe weather, especially those accessing the beach via bicycle and pedestrian modes.

- Traffic management. There are shortcomings in real-time traffic and emergency monitoring (Route 175), special event and peak weekend traffic routing, real-time traffic and parking information for visitors (internet, radio, variable message signs), off-site pass pre-purchasing, and pre-trip planning information via electronic media. These all contribute to road congestion and negative visitor experience and air quality impacts.

- Parking management. In addition to the real-time information shortfalls identified above, there is no designated off-site beach parking (satellite or garage) during summer peak days or when beach lot capacity is reduced due to severe weather. Available CNWR maps do not clearly show parking locations and other transportation data needed by visitors.

  The lack of off-site parking limits the potential of transit into CNWR and, in conjunction with limited printed and real-time parking data, causes delays at the fee booths and extra driving in CNWR, leading to congestion, air pollution, and a negative impact on visitor experience.

- Bicycle and pedestrian modes. There are gaps in sidewalks and bike trails and lanes on main thoroughfares between the Town of Chincoteague and CNWR, particularly Maddox Boulevard and a lack of crosswalks and pedestrian signals at key signalized intersections. Bicycle maps and signage are limited, and distribution of outreach materials could be improved.

  These issues degrade safety for bicyclists and pedestrians and are a barrier to increased access by those modes.

- Transit. There is currently no transit service into CNWR, trolleys do not accommodate bicycles or other recreational gear, and Pony Express routes overlap and are long and circuitous.

  Thus, transit does not significantly mitigate beach traffic congestion or offer access to other ASIS and CNWR sites. The service as configured discourages bicycle use and may be limiting ridership.

Summary assessment results, Alternatives 2 through 4

The action alternatives may be seen by decision makers and managers in three ways:

- Integrated system planning options directly corresponding to CCP alternatives;

- A phased approach to funding and implementation of a transportation system serving CNWR and ASIS under the chosen CCP alternative; and

- A menu of transportation solutions, with information on implementation, cost, time requirements and public process, available to planners to fund and implement as appropriate and feasible.

This summary will follow the second approach, in which the action alternatives are viewed as phases that build upon each other and lead to a mature transportation system, as CNWR and ASIS re-evaluate the responsible and sustainable management of the beach parking lots and related infrastructure in light of the present and future effects of climate change, increasing frequency and severity of storms, and rising sea level. In this reckoning, the scenario corresponding to Alternative 2, maintaining the beach parking as is, and continuing to incur the necessary level of operations and maintenance costs, is a temporary phase and addresses three needs:

- Providing low cost, quickly implementable solutions that improve the status quo transportation system;

- Making progress by laying a foundation for the larger scale investments and projects that will be necessary in the future; and

- Allowing time for the planning, design, and identification of funding for the solutions in Alternatives 3 and 4 to proceed.

Alternative 2 comprises many non-controversial, low cost, and relatively simple solutions for traffic management, safety for bicyclists and pedestrians, and improved traveler information. It also includes four higher cost and effort infrastructure projects on the Route 175 Causeway and Maddox Boulevard and a siren notification system at the beach, for which quick implementation is justifiable given their safety and emergency response benefits. It should, however, be noted that the solutions in this alternative do not address or reduce the status quo cost of maintaining the existing beach parking lots.

Alternative 3 provides the transportation system to move visitors between off-site parking facilities and the public beach. It has the most long-term solutions with significant positive effect, including important infrastructure projects that improve safety, traffic management and ITS measures, and the full implementation of satellite parking.

Alternative 4 may be seen as the capstone, with several high capital cost solutions including the construction of a new, off-site parking garage at a suitable site to be determined in the Town of Chincoteague. It also provides for bike lanes on the Route 175 Causeway and Maddox Boulevard, and transit service expansion to serve the parking garage with a fleet of new vehicles built to accommodate beachgoers.

The progressive scale of Alternatives 2 through 4 yields progressively better results with respect to the assessment criteria, as summarized below.

1. Protection and conservation of natural, historic, and cultural resources

The modest scale of solutions in Alternative 2 results in little direct, positive benefit and no significant degradation of resources within ASIS/CNWR.

Alternative 3 has the greatest impact in reducing traffic volume and congestion within ASIS/CNWR, because of its ITS solutions, satellite parking and shuttle service, and completion of the bike trail between the Black Duck trail and the beach. Alternative 4 would offer an incremental, but less dramatic, impact. Likewise, the reduction of the footprint of parking facilities in ASIS/CNWR as a result of both Alternatives 3 and 4 would be significant.

Infrastructure solutions will bring some physical and aesthetic impact to resources both within and outside of ASIS/CNWR. Alternative 3's fee booth relocation, widened Assateague Channel Bridge, and widened shoulders on the Route 175 Causeway will require planning to mitigate possible negative impacts in adjacent environmentally sensitive areas. Use of existing community and public parking lots for peak seasonal beach parking replaces capacity without any new infrastructure or environmental impact, while reducing the beach parking footprint.

Alternative 4 adds an off-site parking garage that also replaces capacity at the beach parking lots, but its design must be carefully considered to avoid negative impacts elsewhere.

2. Optimization of the transportation system's operational efficiency to improve visitor mobility, safety, and accessibility

Alternative 2 provides many modest public information and fee purchase solutions that will bring some traffic and parking management benefits, but does not substantively address bicycle, pedestrian and transit improvements. Several infrastructure solutions directly address improvement of safety, particularly on the Route 175 Causeway.

Alternative 3 would accommodate the smooth entry of transit vehicles, pre-paid cars, and emergency vehicles into ASIS/CNWR, provide real-time beach parking and traffic information through new ITS features, add transit routing into ASIS/CNWR and new gear accommodations to expand visitor access options for both day trippers and longer term visitors, greatly expand bicycle access on Maddox Boulevard and the Route 175 Causeway, and provide much improved pedestrian and bicycle safety on the Maddox Boulevard approach to ASIS/CNWR

The widening the Route 175 Causeway under Alternative 4 would be a significant safety enhancement, and the garage and associated transit service would reinforce the Alternative 3 transportation system solutions that respond to the off-site beach parking strategy.

3. *Sustainability of transportation system, to minimize congestion and pollution*

Alternative 2 would result in modest reductions in congestion in AIS/CNWR and the Town of Chincoteague, and of tailpipe emissions, and liquid spillage affecting ASIS/CNWR. Alternatives 3 and 4 would significantly reduce peak-time congestion and pollution, mostly due to satellite and garage parking, in concert with ITS and transit solutions.

Alternative 3 would utilize existing parking facilities to replace beach parking capacity, while the parking garage in Alternative 4 would require careful siting and design to minimize open space and other impacts in the Town of Chincoteague.

4. *Improvement of the visitor experience, in particular the understanding and appreciation of fish and wildlife resources*

The purpose of improved transportation and access is not to maximize visitation but to improve the visitor's experience of ASIS/CNWR by reducing traffic congestion and delays. Alternative 2 would have a modest beneficial effect through the convenience of information retrieval and pre-purchase of passes, which may also help promote visits to non-beach sites in CNWR.

The infrastructure, parking, bicycle, and traffic solutions in Alternative 3 will significantly improve the visitor's experience, by reducing frustration with bicycle and pedestrian solutions and encouraging more people to visit non-beach sites in ASIS/CNWR. The expanded transit service into CNWR would provide new opportunities for interpretive services.

There would modest incremental benefit due to Alternative 4's transit solutions , which would increase transit ridership into ASIS/CNWR and the audience for new interpretive services.

5. *Fostering and sustaining partnerships*

Alternative 2 lays the groundwork for many new and enhanced partnerships with the ATPPL co-applicants and public and private and private entities, with new information resources and pass purchase opportunities. Alternative 3 builds upon these with significant ITS and off-site visitor information solutions, the transit route extensions, and the management and operation of satellite parking lots. The parking management and transit solutions in Alternative 4 will require the maturation of the partnerships established for the Alternative 3 solutions, notably with the Town, the County, and the Pony Express or other transit service provider.

It is evident, but not quantifiable in the context of this study, that the escalating scope and scale of transportation system improvements in Alternatives 2, 3, and 4 will promote tourism and economic and social benefits in the whole study area, notably the Town of Chincoteague. This effect would be positive for the Town's need to sustain and grow commercial activity and local businesses; however, it illuminates the matter of striking the appropriate balance between commercial interests and the missions of ASIS and CNWR (see further discussion below).

6. *Financial sustainability and cost-effectiveness*

Under Alternative 2, ASIS/CNWR would continue to incur the high operations and maintenance (O & M) costs for the beach parking lots. The solutions therein are mainly low-cost items, with negligible to low O & M costs.

The relocation or size reduction of beach parking lots in Alternative 3 would likely result in a significant reduction of O & M. Otherwise, ASIS/CNWR would have added O & M effort and costs for new infrastructure and some ITS features. The Assateague Channel Bridge widening would require capital funding estimated at nearly $7M. The parking management solutions have low start-up and significant O & M costs for partner entities, particularly personnel and other costs for satellite parking, which may generate offsetting revenue. Bike and pedestrian routing and safety solutions in the Town of Chincoteague would total to nearly $200,000 in capital cost, with minor incremental O & M cost. The extended bus route would add significant O & M costs for the transit operator.

Under Alternative 4, the elimination of beach parking lots would reduce O & M costs more relative to Alternative 3. The new parking garage would have very high start-up and capital costs (estimated at $7.75M) and high O & M costs ($342K per year for a 500-car garage), again with offsetting parking revenue. However, in this alternative a widened Assateague Channel Bridge is not required. The Route 175 Causeway widening is also capital-intensive (estimated at $2.8M); however, the incremental O & M costs would be minor for VDOT.

The bus service to the parking garage would not by itself add significant O/M costs for the operator. Two new vehicles would cost $200,000 to -$400,000 each, and alternative fuel vehicles, if chosen, would likely increase O & M cost to accommodate the new technology. However, the extended and improved service would be likely to induce increased ridership and offsetting revenue.

b. Next Steps

Key considerations for CNWR, ASIS, and partners

1. Carrying capacity

CNWR has several important considerations to carry forward from this study into the comprehensive conservation plan (CCP) process. As FWS managers analyze carrying capacity and visitor experience, the essential and constant underlying condition for the CCP alternatives is that net total parking spaces for beachgoers will remain the same, provided by a variety of possible combinations of on-site and off-site parking. That is, the transportation alternatives described in this study aim to supplant rather than supplement private automobiles, with the result that transportation needs for possible increases in future visitation to the beach are served by new and improved alternative modes including transit, bicycle, and pedestrian. However, FWS management has pointed out that the beach's natural habitat and its carrying capacity, both for human and animal visitors, may increase as vehicle parking space there is reduced. The appropriate balance between wildlife management and beach visitation is a key issue for the CCP. The same may be said for other sites in CNWR where visitation may increase as a result of future implementation of transportation solutions.

The other balance that FWS management must address is the CNWR's mission and visitation target as they relate to economic development in the Town and County. The new Route 175 – Maddox Boulevard Bridge in combination with the transportation system improvements suggested herein may induce more visits and tourist activity, a highly desirable outcome in the view of the Town, County, and Chamber of Commerce. However, the Town itself faces some limitations to visitation increase during peak summer months, such as room availability and sewer infrastructure capacity.

2. Parking and fees

ASIS/CNWR will have many operations and financial questions to consider as they move to a new parking management model. Many of the routine operations matters will be worked out as new and enhanced partnerships are developed to provide transit, improved bicycle and pedestrian routes, information sharing, and pass purchase and fee collection methods. The larger operations picture will include some combination of beach, satellite, and garage parking, with the possibility that there will be limited to no beach parking capacity. A number of parking demand scenarios appear in Table 15 to serve as a series of hypothetical examples in which some residual parking capacity is retained at the beach.

Note that the beach and garage capacities are notional; the satellite parking capacity (existing Town and County parking lots) is actual.

Table 15. Future Parking Scenarios.

Parking Asset	Parking demand scenarios			
	Off-peak and off-season	"Shoulder" weekends, some peak weekdays	Peak weekends and holidays	Special events, e.g., Pony Swim
Beach parking (200)	Beach parking alone is adequate.	Beach parking at full capacity.	Beach parking at full capacity.	Beach parking at full capacity.
Garage (300)	No capacity needed.	Garage partially full.	Garage full.	Garage full.
Satellite parking (550)	No capacity needed.	No capacity needed.	Partially to completely full	Completely full. Some net loss of capacity for these events.

Many management and financial questions and fee collection issues will arise with the adoption of a new parking management strategy. The most important of these are:

- What is the appropriate future aggregate capacity of all parking facilities? The commonly used definition of the current capacity only includes the beach parking lots (approximately 1,000 cars). Although existing Town and County lots are sometimes used for special events such as the Pony Swim, they are not now used for peak day summer beach parking. The appropriate planning number for the future may be the "net zero" value of 961, or a greater or lesser number as determined by the CCP process.

- What is the appropriate mix of parking assets? Satellite parking capacities of existing lots in the Town of Chincoteague are known. The key questions are what capacity, if any, to retain at the beach and what the garage capacity will be.

- What will be the appropriate parking and CNWR entry revenue targets, given reduced or eliminated O & M costs for the beach parking lots?

- What is the prospect for the garage to be financially self-sustaining? Even if its capital costs are covered by public appropriation and/or grant money, the O & M costs are significant.

It will be appropriate to analyze several projected demand and revenue scenarios, varying beach (starting at zero) and garage capacities, and based upon year-round daily visitation data. Beach parking alone will bring significant demand for a small number of days per year, with or without the parking lots at the beach. The analysis would therefore also have to examine other possible sources of parking income.

- What will be the ownership and management model for the garage (e.g., Government owned and operated, Government owned-contractor operated, privately owned and operated)? Would a concession be appropriate?

- What will the fee structure be in respect to parking?
  - Will the fees vary for beach, garage and satellite parking to reflect convenience and amenities variables? Will the beach parking fee include an increment for lot O & M costs?

- Will the fees for off-site parking include the CNWR entrance fee, either as a concession fee or bundled purchase? Would the bundled purchase also include a transit fee for those who use the shuttle?

New and enhanced partnerships

A number of short-term recommendations have been identified resulting from the partnership assessment, mainly concerning formalizing relationships and including additional stakeholders in regular activities. The recommendations include:

- Formalize existing relationships by developing memoranda of agreement with:
  - WCTG
  - Chincoteague police (in progress)
  - VDOT (for general technical support as well as traffic camera monitoring and other emergency management response)
- Submit an Advisory Opinion Request Form[54] for proposed emergency service and/or expanded route of Pony Express service to FTA to verify that the service is consistent with charter regulations[55]
- Include additional community leaders in meetings, including representatives of VDOT (District Engineer), Accomack County, Accomack-Northampton Planning District Commission, Chincoteague Cultural Alliance, and the Chincoteague Main Street Association
- Identify an entity or person that can act as a transportation resource for CNWR. Possibilities include the regional Refuge Roads manager for FWS Northeast Region, CNWR or ASIS staff person, Town, County, or VDOT staff person, or FTA/FHWA local office staff.

Future planning study needs

The co-applicants will need to monitor the effectiveness of the transportation solutions that are put in place, through analysis and reiteration of the planning process. To do so, it is critical to collect performance data, starting as early as possible; these efforts should include:

- Data collection and analysis in ASIS/CNWR to characterize visitation and transportation modes to the beach and other sites on a year round basis
- Traffic data collection on key routes in the County and Town, including measurement of seasonal effects, and especially in regard to the effect of the new Route 175 Bridge alignment
- Modal transportation data in the Town of Chincoteague, including bicycles, pedestrians, scooters, and golf carts, through rental data and collection by observers at key points, Maddox Boulevard in particular

Policy matters for co-applicants

Key planning documents by the Town of Chincoteague and VDOT have already identified important transportation policies that align with the solutions found in this report, in regard to bicycle and pedestrian access, safety, and traffic management. There is a small number of additional policy considerations for the future beyond the new partnership activities recommended herein; these are:

---

[54] Advisory Opinion Request Form. http://www.fta.dot.gov/documents/Advisory_Opinion_Form.pdf

[55] In personal communication with Crystal Frederick ((202) 366-4063; ombudsman.charterservice@dot.gov), the transit service options were considered to be consistent with charter regulations.

- Town ordinance to allow golf carts on streets. The thrust of this change would be to remove larger vehicles to reduce congestion and, presumably, to reduce emissions. This ordinance would have to examine several issues closely, including:
    - Safety, including licensing, vehicle standards, operating restrictions (e.g., as in peer example Folly Beach, SC), and the possibility that some carts may wind up in operating in bike lanes
    - Congestion, the benefits for which may be negligible or even negative if additional vehicle use is induced
    - Pollution, which could actually be worse if carts with 2-cycle gas engines are allowed, and the possible restriction to electric carts
- Charging stations for electric cars. This ambitious project could be part of a green solutions initiative. It would require active partnership among Town, County, VDOT, and other partners.
- Consideration of passenger vessel services. The Town of Chincoteague and ASIS/CNWR can in the long term revisit the concept of focused passenger services between the Town and the Lighthouse landing and the old Coast Guard station on Toms Cove Hook. These would be small-scale services, likely run by a local operator as a supplement to an existing service, catering to specialized segments of the visitor population and particular educational, cultural and historic groups.

c. Funding sources

There are several funding sources for transportation through the Fish & Wildlife Service, National Park Service, U.S. DOT Federal Highway Administration (FHWA) and Federal Transit Administration (FTA), and through private sources. Many of the programs are oversubscribed compared to the current need, making them highly competitive. Since CNWR is entirely within FWS and NPS boundaries, FHWA programs that are administered through states or local governments, such as the Transportation Enhancement and Safe Routes to Schools funding sources, typically are ineligible or a viewed as a lesser priority by the primary recipients. However, since access to CNWR and ASIS is dependent on transportation infrastructure within the Town of Chincoteague and Accomack County, CNWR and ASIS should and can partner with state and local entities to pursue funding for regional and local improvements to access to Assateague Island.

Table 16 provides information on some of the primary funding programs; however, the list is not exhaustive. CNWR and ASIS should work with partners and agency funding program staff to identify what funding would be most appropriate for which projects.

Table 16. Funding Sources.

Level	Agency	Funding	Project Eligibility
Federal	FHWA	Federal Lands Highway Program – Discretionary Funding[56]	Wide variety of project types that provide access to or within or adjacent to Federal lands (Transportation planning, research, engineering, and construction of highways, parkways, and transit facilities; also operation and maintenance of transit facilities). Funding is limited and competition is high; State Highway Administrator submits projects.
Federal	FHWA	Emergency Relief for Federally Owned (ERFO) Roads Program[57]	Assistance to repair and reconstruct Federal and Indian roads damaged in a natural disaster over a wide area or by catastrophic failure resulting from external causes.
Federal	FHWA	Refuge Roads Program[58]	Maintenance and improvements to existing roads, trails, and parking lots.
Federal	FHWA	Coordinated Technology Implementation Program (CTIP)[59]	Technology-based projects that meet the following criteria: • Innovative, unique, or underused transportation technology • Doesn't require research • Adds Value • Meets a specific need • Supports public roads or facilities • Costs less than $200,000 • Time frame less than three (3) years
Federal	FHWA / NPS	Federal Lands Highway Program - Park Roads and Parkways Program	Rebuilding of existing road and bridge infrastructure (Category I), construction of Congressionally-authorized parkway projects (Category II), and planning and capital assistance for alternative transportation systems (Category III)
Federal / State	FHWA / Virginia DCR[60]	Recreational Trails Program	Capital and maintenance of both motorized and non-motorized trail use.

---

[56] Office of Federal Lands Highways website. http://flh.fhwa.dot.gov/

[57] Office of Federal Lands Highways website. http://flh.fhwa.dot.gov/

[58] Office of Federal Lands Highways website. http://flh.fhwa.dot.gov/

[59] Coordinated Technology Implementation Program (CTIP) website. http://www.ctiponline.org/submit_proposal/.

[60] Virginia Recreational Trails Program website, http://www.dcr.virginia.gov/recreational_planning/trailfnd.shtml

References

Accomack County. *Respecting the Past, Creating the Future: Accomack County Comprehensive Plan.* May 14, 2008. http://www.co.accomack.va.us/Planning/2008_comprehensive_plan_update.html

Accomack-Northampton Planning District Commission. *Accomack-Northampton (PDC 22) Coordinated Human Service Mobility Plan.* June 2008.

Accomack-Northampton Planning District Commission, Eastern Shore of Virginia Bicycle Committee. *Eastern Shore of Virginia Bicycle Plan.* March 2004. http://www.a-npdc.org/esvbicycleplan2004.pdf

Accomack-Northampton Planning District Commission. *Eastern Shore of Virginia Comprehensive Economic Development Strategy.* April 2004. http://www.esva.net/~accomack/Board%20of%20Supervisors/Agendas/Prior%20Agendas/M-2007-12-19/County%20Administration%20YNP%20AC1%20A1.pdf

Assateague Island National Seashore. *General Management Plan.* June 1982.

Barry Lawson Associates, Inc. *Analysis of Traffic Management Options.* June 1986.

Carver, Erin, and James Caudill. *Banking on Nature 2006: The Economic Benefits to Local Communities of National Wildlife Visitation.* U.S. Fish and Wildlife Service, Division of Economics. September 2007. http://www.fws.gov/refuges/about/pdfs/BankingOnNature2006_1123.pdf

Chincoteague National Wildlife Refuge. www.fws.gov/refuges/profiles/index.cfm?id=51570

Chincoteague National Wildlife Refuge. *Alternative Transportation in Parks and Public Lands Program Project Proposal: Conduct a comprehensive transportation plan.* 2007.

Chincoteague National Wildlife Refuge. *Alternative Transportation in Parks and Public Lands Program Project Proposal: Construct Pedestrian/Bike Trail.* 2008.

Chincoteague National Wildlife Refuge. *Alternative Transportation in Parks and Public Lands Program Project Proposal: Provide Intelligent Information Traffic Systems.* 2008.

Chincoteague Reports. November 5, 2007 Town Council Meeting http://www.chincoteaguereports.com/my_weblog/chincoteague-town-council/page/2/

Chincoteague Reports. January 18, 2007 Town Council Meeting. http://www.chincoteaguereports.com/my_weblog/2007/01/january_18_2007.html

Chincoteague Reports. December 3, 2007 Town Council Meeting. http://www.chincoteaguereports.com/my_weblog/chincoteague-town-council/page/2/

Commonwealth of Virginia. *Hurricane Response Plan: Basic Plan – Appendix I: Hurricane Hazards and History.* http://www.vaemergency.com/library/plans/hurrplan/09_hurricane_respons_plan/Basic%20Plan%20Appendix%20I%20-%20June%202009.pdf

Commonwealth of Virginia. *Emergency Operations Plan: Hurricane Response Plan Annex B – Appendix I.* http://www.vaemergency.com/library/plans/hurrplan/09_hurricane_respons_plan/Annex%20B%20Appendix%20I%20-%20June%202009.pdf

Defenders of Wildlife. *Refuges at Risk: The Threat of Global Warming.* 2006. http://www.defenders.org/resources/publications/programs_and_policy/science_and_economics/global_warming/refuges_at_risk_2006.pdf

Eppley Institute for Parks and Public Lands, Indiana University. *Assateague Island National Seashore Visitor Survey.* January 16, 2007.

Federal Highway Administration, Central Federal Lands Highway Division. Guide to Promoting Bicycling on Federal Lands. September 2008. www.westerntransportationinstitute.org

Federal Highway Administration and Federal Transit Administration. *Federal Lands Alternative Transportation Study: Field Report – Chincoteague National Wildlife Refuge.* 2001.

Furness, Stephen. *Chincoteague Beacon.* December 9, 2004.

Furness, Stephen. "Refuge will experiment with hotel taxi services." *Chincoteague Beacon.* May 12, 2005.

Furness, Stephen. "Trolley season a success official says." *Chincoteague Beacon.* November 3, 2005.

Furness, Stephen. Boy, 11, dies in causeway crash." *Chincoteague Beacon.* August 8, 2007.

Furness, Stephen. "Council will continue with trolleys." *Chincoteague Beacon.* February 5, 2008.

Governor's Commission on Climate Change. *Final Report: A Climate Change Action Plan.* December 15, 2008 http://www.deq.state.va.us/export/sites/default/info/documents/climate/CCC_Final_Report-Final_12152008.pdf

Interagency Transportation Assistance Group. *Transportation Observations, Considerations and Recommendations for the Chincoteague National Wildlife Refuge (TAG Report).* April 2007.

Keer, Ann R. *Environmental Planning Analysis: For Traffic Management of Chincoteague National Wildlife Refuge.* Salisbury State University. Undated.

Land Studio PC. Chincoteague Streetscape Enhancement Project. http://www.landstudiopc.com/Chincoteague_Clients_Page.html

Louis Berger Group, Inc. *Chesapeake Bay Bridge-Tunnel Commuter Toll Impact Study.* Prepared for: Chesapeake Bay Bridge-Tunnel Commuter Toll Impact Study Committee. October 2001. http://www.a-npdc.org/cbbt.htm

National Oceanic and Atmospheric Administration, Chesapeake Bay Office. "Climate Change and the Chesapeake Bay: FAQ." July 2008. http://chesapeakebay.noaa.gov/docs/FAQClimateChangeinCB8.08.pdf

National Park Service Public Use Statistics Office. http://www.nature.nps.gov/stats

National Wildlife Federation. *Sea Level Rise and Coastal Habitats in the Chesapeake Bay Region.* May 2008. http://www.nwf.org/Global-Warming/Effects-on-Wildlife-and-Habitat/Estuaries-and-Coastal-Wetlands/~/media/PDFs/Global%20Warming/Reports/FullSeaLevelRiseandCoastalHabitats_Chesapeake Region.ashx

Nieves, Delissa Padilla. *Application of the Sea-Level Affecting Marshes Model (SLAMM 5.0.2) in the Lower Delmarva Peninsula (Northampton and Accomack counties, VA / Somerset and Worcester counties, MD).* National Wildlife Refuge System Conservation Biology Program. Arlington, VA. August 26, 2009.

Orbital Sciences Corporation. "Orbital Selected by NASA For $1.9 Billion Space Station Cargo Delivery Contract." 23 December 2008. http://www.orbital.com/NewsInfo/release.asp?prid=680

Panther Motors, Inc. website. http://www.scootcoupe.com

Potter, Mike, John Provo, Sibel Atasoy, Eric Howard, and Charlotte Anders. *Community Economic Development for the Eastern Shore: Summit Report.* Virginia Tech, Office of Economic Development. August 2007. http://www.a-npdc.org/ESVAFinRep2007.pdf

Rocky Mountain Climate Organization and the Natural Resources Defense Council. *National Parks in Peril: The Threats of Climate Change Disruption – State Fact Sheet: Maryalnd Virginia.* 2009. http://www.rockymountainclimate.org/website%20pictures/ParksinPeril_MD-VAFacts.pdf

Town of Chincoteague. *Chincoteague Comprehensive Plan.* April 2009. http://www.chincoteague-va.gov/municipal/pdf/DRAFT%20COMP%20PLAN%2011_06.pdf

Town of Chincoteague. *Chincoteague Comprehensive Plan.* December 2006. http://www.chincoteague-va.gov

Town of Chincoteague Newsletter. January 14, 2009. http://www.chincoteague-va.gov/announcements/January%20Newsletter%2009.pdf.

Town of Chincoteague: Pony Swim Shuttle Information. http://www.chincoteague-va.gov/visitors/pony%20swim%20shuttle%20stop%20map.shtm

Town of Chincoteague. *Bicycle Plan.* From Meeting Notes of the Recreation & Community Enhancement Committee Meeting, May 19, 2009.

Town of Chincoteague website. http://www.chincoteague-va.gov/

Town of Chincoteague. Public Planning Workshop Results. January 27, 2005.

U.S. Army Corps of Engineers. Delmarva Hurricane Evacuation Study Draft Storm Surge Map/Evacuation Zone Map (Draft August 2006). http://www.nap.usace.army.mil/HES/Delmarva/maps/ACCOMACK_VUL_HU_06AUGUST07.pdf

United States Census. 2000. U.S. Census Bureau.

U.S. Environmental Protection Agency. "A Case Study on Chesapeake Bay and Assateague Island." 2001 Climate Change, Wildlife, and Wildlands Toolkit. http://www.epa.gov/climatechange/wycd/downloads/CS_Ches.pdf

U.S. Environmental Protection Agency. *Coastal Sensitivity to Sea-level Rise: A Focus on the Mid-Atlantic Region.* January 15, 2009. http://www.climatescience.gov/Library/sap/sap4-1/final-report/sap4-1-final-report-FrontMatter.pdf

U.S. Fish & Wildlife. *Master Plan: Chincoteague National Wildlife Refuge.* December 1993.

Chincoteague National Wildlife Refuge. www.fws.gov/refuges/profiles/index.cfm?id=51570

U.S. Fish and Wildlife Service. National Refuge System Website. 2009. http://www.fws.gov/refuges/

US Fish & Wildlife Service Refuge Planning: Northeast Region. What are CCP's? http://www.fws.gov/northeast/planning/whatareccps.html

Vaughn, Carol. "Wrecks don't qualify causeway for upgrades." *The Daily Times.* November 21, 2007.

Vaughn, Carol. "Accomack Board Denies Bike Lane Study Despite Boy's Death." *The Daily Times.* December 21, 2007. http://www.vabike.org/accomac-denies-bike-lane-study/

Virginia Department of Motor Vehicles: Virginia Crash Facts, http://www.dmv.state.va.us/webdoc/safety/crash_data/crash_facts/index.asp

Virginia Department of Rail and Public Transportation. *FY2003 Public Transportation Improvement Program.* http://www.drpt.virginia.gov/studies/files/DRPT-FY03-ProgramOfProjects.pdf

Virginia Department of Rail and Public Transportation. *DRPT Six Year Improvement Plans.* http://www.drpt.virginia.gov/about/finance.aspx

Virginia Department of Rail and Public Transportation. *FY2006 Rail and Public Transportation Improvement Program.* http://www.drpt.virginia.gov/studies/files/DRPT-FY06-ProgramOfProjects.pdf

Virginia Department of Transportation. *2025 State Highway Plan.*
http://virginiadot.org/projects/resources/Virginia2025StateHighwayPlanTechReport.pdf

Virginia Department of Transportation. "Chincoteague Bridge Replacement."

http://www.virginiadot.org/projects/hamptonroads/chincoteague_bridge_replacement.asp

Virginia Department of Transportation. *Chincoteague Visitor Transportation Study.* December 1998.

Virginia Department of Transportation. *Route 13/Wallops Island Access Management Study.* May 2002.
http://virginiadot.org/projects/resources/hampton_roads/rte13_final_report.pdf

Virginia Department of Transportation. Rural Regional Long-Range Plans.

http://virginiadot.org/projects/rural_regional_long-range_plans.asp

Virginia Department of Transportation, U.S. Department of Transportation Federal Highway
Administration, and the Town of Chincoteague. *Chincoteague 2020 Transportation Plan.* August 2002.
http://www.virginiadot.org/projects/resources/Chincoteague_plansummary_FINAL.pdf

Vollmer Associates. *Transportation Study: Assateague Island.* June 1976.